STORMY SEAS WE BRAVE

STORMY SEAS WE BRAVE

Creative Expressions by Uprooted People

Compiled by Helene Moussa

WCC Publications, Geneva

Cover photo

Artist's name: Phi Thi Minh Ha. 32 year old Vietnamese refugee in High Island, North Camp, Hong Kong. The painting was done in July 1990 at the Garden Stream "Art in the Camp" project that ran art and crafts programmes inside the detention centre from 1988-1993. Garden Streams is a Hong Kong Fellowship of Christian Artists.

Photo taken by Garden Streams.

ISBN 2-8254-1281-3

©1998 World Council of Churches
150 route de Ferney
1211 Geneva 2
Switzerland

Printed in Switzerland

Design and lay out by Edwin Hassink

TABLE OF CONTENTS

STORMY SEAS WE BRAVE

INTRODUCTION

This collection of poems, lyrics, reflections, dramas and
photographic reproductions of sculptures, paintings, drawings and
embroidery by uprooted people (refugees, internally displaced
persons and migrants) celebrates their creativity, resilience and
courage. The voices in this collection remind us to look beyond
public statements and policies, academic discourses, statistics,
media images and those who write or speak about uprooted
people. The reader is invited to listen to the innermost being of
uprooted people, to their perspectives, to their hopes, dreams and
visions, to their feelings of loss and suffering, to their fears,
despair and doubts, to their anger and to the love and joy they
yearn for and share. Uprooted people express here their acute
understanding of the violence that has "produced" them. Their
political insights challenge us to ask different questions. The
material in this collection is deeply personal. To engage with it is
provocative.

The contributors to this collection are uprooted people from all
regions of the world. They are people who have sought refuge
within their own countries, in neighbouring countries and in
regions other than their own. They are people who have had to flee
from their communities or countries because of war, civil conflict,
human rights violations, genocide. They are people who have been

displaced because of colonization of land and resources and the severe breakdown of economic and social conditions that made survival in traditional communities impossible. Some of the contributors are spouses or children of uprooted people.

The idea of this collection was conceived from feedback to drafts of the WCC Policy Statement on Uprooted People (1995) and accompanying Resource Book.[1] Members of our constituency posed the challenge that we are always writing about the poor, the oppressed, uprooted people; why can we not turn to uprooted people's understandings of their experience(s) and the expression of their own spirituality? This challenge made me realize once again how my own journey and ministry has been enlightened by uprooted people I have had the privilege of knowing and being in solidarity with their search for justice and in their struggles to re-build their lives. Often in my relationships with uprooted people, I have had the opportunity to hear, see and read their creative expressions in song, art and poetry. These moments have not only touched me deeply but made me conscious how creative expressions reveal very different dimensions of the experience of uprooting and enable their creators (irrespective of age) to communicate what might be more difficult in conversation or in formal writing.

While uprooted people are ripped up from their homelands, the contributors in this collection express their struggle to nourish their roots at the same time as they try to re-build their lives. Feelings of homesickness or longing for the familiar environment are ways of maintaining what is valued from the past while at the same time searching to belong in the new environment. Remembering is part of the process of re-constructing their lives despite the "storms" that uprooted them.

A number of the contributors said that they chose to express themselves through art form as a healing and survival processes and/or to advocate for human rights. As Sudharshana Coomarasamy (refugee from Sri Lanka) said to me: "Writing has in one sense been a journey of discovery of self and of transforming pain into poetry." The letter attaching a play written and produced by children born of Japanese fathers and Filipina mothers working in Japan stated: "Nothing is more beautiful than the human capacity to distill pain into something beautiful, and no one is perhaps as blessed as those who witness the transformation of suffering into beauty. Indeed, the souls at the Batis Centre for Women in the Philippines are thus blessed."

Several contributors were established artists before they were forced to leave their homes, communities and country. One of them explained that he was a musician in his home country and that he started to write poetry when he became a refugee because he did not have the financial resources to re-establish himself as a musician. Several of these artists in exile encouraged or taught other uprooted people to express themselves through the medium of art. Products of their students are also included in this collection.

The title of this collection is adapted from a song composed by a Tamil refugee in India (Chapter II). It reflects figuratively and literally the "storms" uprooted people have endured in their journey towards safety and their courage and determination when becoming and being uprooted. The contributors in the collection challenge us and are challenged by the limitations of legal constructs of "refugee", "asylum-seeker", "internally displaced person" and "migrant worker" and the stereotypes and prejudices associated with these labels. They search to maintain their identities and all that they cherish as they re-build their lives. They testify to the horrors of repression, human rights violations and genocide. They condemn the destructiveness and meaninglessness of war and militarization, the divisiveness of political, religious and ethnic domination; and the oppressiveness of economic strategies that put profit over human dignity and the right to development. They advocate for the right to live in safety and human dignity and to lead productive personal and public lives. And despite the many "storms" they continue to weather, they affirm the importance of joining hands to create a world built on values of peace and love with justice.

Over 80 individual responses were received to our invitation to contribute to a collection of creative expressions by uprooted people. Several respondents sent multiple contributions — some as many as 30 individual works by one or more uprooted persons. Each of these could have been independent collections! Most of the contributions in this collection have never been published, although a few have appeared in books, journals or grassroots newsletters. While I have not attempted to have a representation from all countries where people have and are being uprooted, the material includes contributions from all regions.

Contributors to this collection were invited to send their creative works in their language of origin with translations into one of the WCC's official languages. Because of the overwhelming number of responses, a very difficult choice was made to have English as the language of the collection. Contributions in French, German or Spanish have been included together with an English translation. Clearly this decision risked losing much of the essence of the original work. However, I hope that it will result in presenting these voices to a wider audience. A number of contributions were also received in English even though this is not the authors' mother tongue, let alone their second or third language. Two exceptions were made to include contributions (one in Tibetan and one in Arabic) that were submitted in calligraphic style.

Organizing the contributions in this collection under the five thematic chapters is clearly my own interpretation of the material, and represents my desire to present uprooted people in dialogue with each other and as shapers of their lives despite their victimization. The voices in this collection command respect rather than pity or a romanticized admiration. Where information about the authors and/or interpretation have been offered, these have been included. Otherwise each work expresses the particular reality of its creator. Together they weave a picture of the human condition and its contradictions. The reader can only come away with a deeper insight of what it means to be uprooted and the resilience of the human spirit, and be inspired by the power to renew and blessed to struggle together for hope.

1 *Helene Moussa and Patrick Taran, A* Moment to Choose: Risking to be with Uprooted People — a Resource Book, *Geneva, WCC, Refugee and Migration Service, 1996.*

Acknowledgements

I am greatly indebted to many people for making possible this collection of creative expressions by uprooted people. Far too many have collaborated in its production to name them individually.

Special appreciation is extended to national, regional and global ecumenical and religious organizations, grassroots services and advocacy groups and all individuals who responded the invitation to send us artistic expressions by uprooted people.

My deepest gratitude is extended to each of the contributors in this collection. Many uprooted people personally responded to the invitation. Their enthusiasm to have their works in the collection was both encouraging and humbling. I hope that I have honoured their expectations and regret that we could not include all their contributions.

I am grateful to editors and publishers of books, journals and newsletters for the permission to reproduce the works in this collection.

A special "thank you" is extended to many people, including the authors, who translated the works from their original language and their efforts to uphold the essence of the texts.

My heartfelt thanks go to WCC colleagues, many friends, my brother Farag and Laurence Deona who alerted me to potential contributors, generously gave of their time to reflect with me at various stages of the publication, and facilitated the selection process by interpreting the original language of several contributions. Many thanks to Jacqueline Campbell who typed all the texts we received. And last but not least, special appreciation is extended to Doris Appel for her untiring enthusiasm and commitment and the many skills she so willingly offers.

CHAPTER ONE
CHALLENGING IDENTITIES

TO BE AN ARMENIAN

So many times
I have been asked:
What does Armenian mean?

... Being an Armenian
is having an obsession
for the world to know
how hard it is to survive
with the memories
of our lost ones
still fresh and vivid
in the folds of our minds.

It is almost to be a dreamer
waiting
to touch the dream.
It is a ritual
to drop our tears
and root our sweat
in foreign soils.
It is to understand
deep in our bones
the unfairness
of humankind
who denies us the chance
to be revived
in our rights.

It is to climb the soul
to reach the truth
or to fight the injustice
encircling the planet
at large.

The Armenian
is the one who has lost
somewhere
in the burning corners
of the deserts
those who shared
the same poem
the same blood.

The one who knows
the meaning of being
tortured and enslaved
and how to be chained
to the roots of an end.

The special one
who has inherited the glory
of a past but is nailed
to the silence of history.

I know it.
I am one of them.

And I can explain with
wounds still open the
screams that roar
inside us.
How can memory erase
a massacre?
How can we save the
innocents thrown into
hell
elders
women
children all of them
with their throats
slashed in the middle
of a song.

We exist here and now
but just in halves
as we also belong there
where old voices are
still haunting us.

We dance and laugh in
fragments as tragedies
are stored in us.

But we believe in
resurrection.
We believe in new
songs and new prayers
in dressing God with
another robe where the
stains of blood will
never show.

We can be born again
from our ashes.

We have the power
to renew
inspire
create
struggle
and fight.
Simply and forever
we are Armenian.

ALICIA GHIRAGOSSIAN

Born in Argentina to Armenian parents survivors of the 1915 genocide, Dr Ghiragossian's poetry has earned international prizes. Lawyer and poet, she writes in Armenian, Spanish, English. She is the author of thirty-eight volumes of poetry which have been translated and published in Italian, Persian, Greek, French, Arabic, Russian and Portuguese (reprinted from Al-Raida, XIV, no. 78, summer 1997, pp.38-39).

NATIVITY

AUGUSTINO F. ALIKUTEPA

41-year old refugee from Mozambique in Kenya

LAS LENGUAS
DE MI TIERRA

Guatemala tierra linda
tú pareces un jardín
muchas lenguas son tus flores
su perfume es para ti.

Te saludo en jakalteco
te enamoro en Tzutuhil
yo te abrazo en castellano
y te beso en lengua ixil.

En quiché me das la mano
y me miras en q'eqchí
q'anjob'al es tu sonrisa
y en mam me dices sí.

**Ay, ay, ay, que alegre estoy
ya parece volando voy,
Guatemalita de mi vida
cuando habrá en ti libertad.**

Guatemalita combativa
viene el hombre engañador
el querrá que tú lo abraces
cualquier lengua por igual.

Su dialecto busca siempre
la palabra división
vele bien sus verdes ojos
no te puede dar amor.

Ya con esta me despido
ya parece volando voy
Guatemalita de mi vida
Cuando habrá en ti libertad.

THE LANGUAGES
OF MY LAND

Guatemala, fairest land,
you are like a garden.
Your many languages are its flowers,
and their scent is for your delight.

I greet you in Jakalteco.
I express my love for you in Tzutuhil.
I hug you in Castilian.
And I kiss you in Ixil.

You shake my hand in Quiché.
You gaze on me in Q'eqchí.
Your smile is Q'anjob'al.
You say "yes" to me in Mam.

**Oh, oh, oh, how happy I am.
I feel as if I have wings.
sweet Guatemala, love of my life,
when freedom will be yours.**

Sweet Guatemala, as you fight,
beware, a deceiver comes.
He will want you to embrace him,
accept all languages as the same.

In his dialect he is for ever
seeking out the word "division".
Look well at his green eyes.
He cannot give you love.

And so I bid farewell.
I feel as if I have wings,
sweet Guatemala, love of my life,
when freedom will be yours.

*Comunidades de Población en
Resistencia, «Comunidad Prima-
vera Del Ixcán», Finca San Isidor,
Ixcán, Quiché, Guatemala, C.A.*

*People's Resistance Communities,
Springtime Community of Ixcán
San Isidro Estate, Ixcán, Quiché,
Guatemala, Central America.*

None Better than My Land

I have eaten in America
I have been to Australia
I have changed my ways in Fiji
I have been mobbed in Guam
I have cooked in the Cook Islands
I have sneezed in the Marshall Islands
I have damaged what was on Nauru
I have fainted in New Caledonia
I have woken up to a New Zealand dawn
I have fried fish in Japan
I have eaten fish in the Solomon Islands
I have tempted fish in Tuvalu
I have been lost in Vanuatu

I have toured many lands
And I saw that my land has nothing

They are sandy, not fertile
But some have black humus soil
they are scorched by the sun
they are spread over Mother Ocean
Like lost children they are lonely
Oh, but how I love them!
My love is wide like Mother Ocean
Broad like their father the Sky
and is rooted firmly to the earth below

I have wandered far and wide
I know very well that my land has nothing
Its beauty lies within me
Not on its surface or wherever
There is none better than my land
None

Teweiariki Francis Teaero
*A native of Kiribati, currently
lecturing at the Department of
Education Psychology of the
University of South Pacific, Fiji
(translated from Kiribati by the
author)*

It is very human to love and
be loved. The individual
I-Kiribati expresses this in
his/her mutual affinity with
the extended family, their
community orientation and
their devotion to the land.
This poem also refers to both
land and people and, in
addition, indirectly refers to
the adopted homeland where
there are beautiful flowers
but which still does not
compare to home.

DESIRE

if i had a pen
if i had a brush
i would pen an image
paint my soul
drown myself
in the beauty
of my land

TEWEIARIKI FRANCIS TEAERO,
FIJI, 1993
*This poem highlights the love of an
intimate closeness to the land. Such
closeness is typical of all I-Kiribati.
This is exemplified by the habit of
the I-Kiribati to identify themselves
with the island where they have
their kaatinga (piece of land in the
village where families have their
home) even if they have not set foot
on that island for a long time, if at
all!*

"Abau" is usually translated
as land. "Bwabwaku" and
"tiara" are two white flowers.
Because of their sweet-
smelling scent, they are
commonly used in making
scented oil. The bwabwaku
flower when woven as a
garland for important guests
is known as an itera. It is
worn only during important
functions and celebrations.

abau
my islands
garland of the gods
woven from fragrant
bwabwaku and *tiare*
dropped carefree
over the big blue
mother oceania

abau
my islands
warmed by the sun
cooled by the moon
caressed by the wind
washed by waves
roused by rain
always

Near East Council of Churches, Committee for Refugees, Gaza

"Nostalgia"
Kamal Mahmoud Moghanni, 1992

Palestine

Taghrid Nabulsi
18-year old Palestinian living in a refugee camp in Lebanon (translated from Arabic by Arab Information Centre for Popular Arts, Lebanon)

I feel that you are a distant dream
I cannot hold or embrace
I feel like a tortured soul
Lost between the hard reality
and the limitless fantasy

1995

NOSTALGIA · HOMESICKNESS · LONGING

Tibetan poem

The snow mountain high above in the blue sky;
Blue river flows on the infinite pasture of Tibet;
And the magnificent Yak (1) takes comfort on the grassland;
Just as if paradise existed in this wide world.

KUNCHOK GYATSO
32-year old refugee from Tibet in
Dharamsala, North India

(1) The yak is the national animal of Tibet.

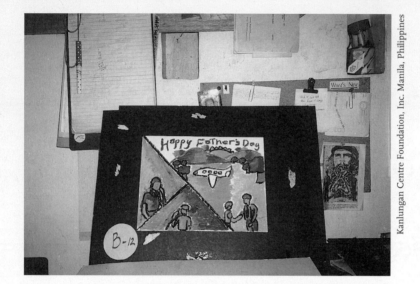

Happy Father's Day

Christopher Tolesa

Special-entry prize-winner in the 12-15 age-group at the 1997 art
competition co-sponsored by Kanlungan Centre Foundation, Inc.
and the National Commission of Culture and Arts, Philippines.
The Kalungan Centre is a migrant workers crisis centre for family
members who remain in the Philippines. Children were asked to
draw on the theme "How do you say 'Happy Father's Day' when
you have not seen him for months and he is a thousand miles
away?"

Filipino, My Fellow Seaman

A seaman is an officer, mechanic, mate
Each to his own task on board, eight hours in all
Toil like a horse to sustain the family
Overtime pay for personal expenses, think hard
Your life depends on this.

Refrain from quarrelling with fellow mates, we are all salary workers
Talk to your equal need not be said, respectful subordinates
Do not lick the boots of the foreigner, the dignity of the Filipino
You must preserve.

Cheap talk and boasting you must avoid, and if at work your knowledge
is lacking
Seek solidarity as brothers and friends, bicker and brawl nowhere will
lead you all
Take care of relationship with officers and mates, to avoid quarrelling
Forgive me, friend, if my words hurt you, but I ask you to reflect on
these.

2/Mate Angel B. Cagwing, Jr. *Kababayan, November 1996*
(reprinted from Parola, no. 81, July-August 1986)

MOTHER AND CHILD (1997)

TIN AUNG WIN (AGED BETWEEN 12 AND 18)

Refugee from Karen state, Myanmar, in Huay Ka Loke refugee camp inside Thailand. This drawing was done "...a few weeks after the Burmese military crossed into Thailand and burned their camps and all their possessions to the ground".

The Future Seems All Dark

VOICE OF A SOUTH SUDANESE CHILD

Mother, Mother, Mother today you are everything to me !!
All responsibilities are on you! Where is father?
I try to locate, can't see his image
The future seems all dark, what next?

Mother, Mother, Mother you always hope to
see father, but see him no more.
Only his spirit seems to exist so!!
The future seems all dark, what next?

Mother, Mother, Mother your heart is full of wounds
as you see your children die of lack of necessities
You can't help, the future seems all dark, what next?

Mother, Mother, Mother you undergo all sorts of
sufferings! Which have no end!
In the process, we end up losing you!
No Mother. No Father, where are we!
The future seems all dark, what next?

Mother, Mother, Mother may the Lord grant you the heart
of perseverance.
The future seems all dark, what next?   *(July 1997)*

HELEN ACHIRO LOTARA   *Sudanese refugee in Kenya, active in a local NGO called Woman Aid. She tries to set up*
Nairobi, July 1997   *programmes for women refugees and displaced. She has several children and struggles to*
                         support them without a husband.

St Andrews African Arts and Crafts Programme, Cairo, Egypt

African Dancer

Ehab Awad Morgan

"I painted this to not forget African festivals." Ehab Awad Morgan is a refugee from Southern Sudan in Egypt, born in 1971. He studied at the Institute of Arts in Sudan before coming to Cairo in 1994. He uses many mediums, among them water colour, oil paint, ink and collage. He sometimes paints cartoon-style characters. His works have been displayed in Sudan and in Cairo.

Le vieil oiseau

Meurtri par le souvenir des belles
scènes d'antan,
Par le vertige, la déchéance,
le silence et souffrant
Moi le Vieil Oiseau,
n'ayant plus le moindre courage,
Esseulé à l'intérieur de cette cage
Où jours et nuits sont confondus,
Je n'ai plus un seul oiseau :
tous se sont envolés et ont disparu.
Mais, quel oiseau pourrait
sans moi dans les airs planer?
Et qui a appris aux autres
la moindre volée
Et la surprise d'une proie?
N'est-ce pas moi?
N'est-ce pas moi?
Dites : qui vous a mis dans le bec
les premiers grains?
Vous n'aviez rien : pas un petit
grain pour calmer la faim.
Le tonnerre a grondé et les autres
oiseaux m'ont abandonné,
Me laissant déplumé;
Pendant combien de temps?
Pour toujours?
Souris et serpents rôdent
tous les jours
Autour de ce nid,
Attirés par mes pattes pourries.

SAMATY HOUNDJOGBÉ
32 ans, réfugié du Togo au Ghana

The Old Bird

Grieved by the remembrance of
the beautiful scenes of yore
By dizziness, fall,
silence and suffering,
Me the old bird,
without the least courage,
Alone in this cage
Where days and nights
are confused,
No bird is left: they all
flew away and disappeared.
But which bird could without me
in the air soar?
And who taught the others
the least flight?
And how to surprise a prey?
Is it not me?
Is it not me?
Say: who put in your beaks
the first grains?
You had nothing: Not the smallest
grain to soothe the hunger.
It thundered and the other birds
abandoned me.
Leaving me plucked.
For how long?
For ever?
Mice and snakes prowl every day
Around this nest
Attracted by my rotten paws.

SAMATY HOUNDJOGBÉ
32 years old, refugee from Togo in Ghana
(translated by the author)

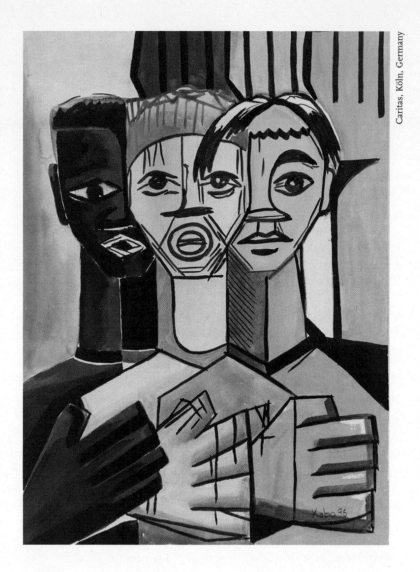

MANY PEOPLE - ONE HEART

KOKOU LAURENT-KABO, 1996
34-year old refugee from Lomé, Togo, in Germany

Don't Call Me a Stranger
The cry of a migrant

Don't call me a stranger:
the language I speak sounds different,
but the feelings it expresses are
the same.

Don't call me a stranger:
I need to communicate,
specially when language is not understood.

Don't call me a stranger:
I need to be together,
specially when
loneliness cools my heart.

Don't call me a stranger:
I need to feel at home,
specially when mine is
very far away from yours.

Don't call me a stranger:
I need a family, because mine
I've left to work for yours.

Don't call me a stranger:
The soil we step on is the same,
but mine is not "the promised land".

Don't call me a stranger:
the colour of my passport is different,
but the colour of our blood is the same.

Don't call me a stranger:
I toil and struggle in your land,

and the sweat of our brows is
the same.

Don't call me a stranger:
borders, we created them,
and the separation that results
is the same.

Don't call me a stranger:
I am just your friend,
but you do not know me yet.

Don't call me a stranger:
we cry for justice and peace in
different ways, but our God is the same.

Don't call me a stranger:
Yes! I am a migrant
but our God is the same.
Amen !

Comboni Missionaries of the Heart of Jesus, Quezon City, Philippines
reprinted from World Mission, March 1995, no. 3

No More Proud

I was so proud of my identity,
like a great king
Who is honoured by his country.
With respectable history,
And being one of
The race that comes early,
Belongs to the land of many streams
Which come through the
Deep heart of big mountains
Flowing with milk and honey.
No one knowing of sadness,
But harmony,
From century to century
Like ancient times
Scriptured in Old Testament.
But after the wind was gone
towards the west
The sun Darkened
and never rose again in the east.
Things turned over
Shaded.
The flow of milk and honey changed
To tears and blood
No more harmony,
and neither bridegroom nor bride
But an everlasting sadness
In the land of Millions
No meadows and green grains
But war fields and naked swords
Against one another
No one remembers his own history
No more proud of self-identity
And no more hope for sanctuary.

Tsegaye Tesfaye
Ethiopian refugee in Kakuma
Refugee Camp, Kenya

reprinted from Kanebu – Kakuma
News Bulletin, March-April 1996,
newsletter published in Kakuma
Refugee Camp, Turkana District,
Kenya, pp.12-13

MAN WITH NO COUNTRY

VAZIRI MOHSEN, FROM TEHERAN, IRAN

SO THEY TELL ME

"You know you look exactly like your grandmother.
You have her eyes, her hair and her smile"
So my Mama and Baba say.
They tell me I remind them of her.
They say whenever I laugh, I speak, they see her in me.

"Oh! This tree, doesn't it look exactly like the one
we had at home." My Mama and Baba tell each other.
They say it reminds them of all the happy times
they spent at home, sitting under the tree with all their family

They remember the stories they used to tell each other,
the songs they sang while roasting maize on the fire,
the dances they danced, the stars they counted, and
the dreams they had.

But I cannot share in their memories.
I do not remember the tree nor the happy times
under the tree.
I was too young to remember so they say,
I ask Mama and Baba – Why can't we just sit under any tree
and do all the things they used to do back home?

"Oh, poor child, they say – it won't be the same.
It is just the three of us here.
Nothing can be the same without your grandparents,
without your uncles, aunts, cousins, neighbours and
all the people we know."

But why are we here all alone – Why are we not with
the rest of the family? I always ask.
And they tell me it is because we are refugees.
Why are we refugees? Why can't we go home? I ask them.

"We ran away from our country because there were
many problems," they tell me.

What problems?
And the answer I get is always the same.
"Child! You are still too young to understand.
You will understand more as you grow." So they say.

I am lucky, at least I have both my parents.
My friend over there has his mother only.
"Your father is in Heaven. He is O.K."
So they tell him. But he doesn't understand
why, and neither do I.
Oh, there are so many things I do not understand.

Yesterday, it was my birthday.
I am now ten years old.
My Mama said, "child you are growing very fast.
Oh if only we were back at home.
How we would celebrate your Birthday.
I would bake our traditional bread and make our
drink, cook our food, just like it has been done for
generations and we would sing and dance and be happy."

What bread, like the one we buy from the shop?
What drink? What food?
Is it different from what we eat here? What music, you
mean using the guitar? I ask.
My mother's eyes water. "My dear, you do not even know
our food. You have never tasted it.
I can't make it here. I do not have all the ingredients.
And the music, the instruments we have are so different.
My child, you are becoming a foreigner to us.
You do not understand when we talk of the old days.
We are losing you." So she tells me.

But Mama, how can I understand all the things you tell
me about – stories you tell me about our country, our
village, our food, music, clothes, family, culture and
even our language.
Mama is it my fault that I do not know these things,
that they don't mean much to me!

I only try to speak our language with you and Baba,
but I am not with you all day – I am almost the
whole day in school where no one knows our language.

When I come home I play with my friends
who do not speak our language either.

I am not proud of my culture,
I do not know the language well,
I cannot cook the food,
I can't play our music – I am lost – So you tell me.
But Mama and Baba, how can I be proud of my
culture when I do not know it?

I grew up here, I know only what I see here every
day, what I eat here every day.
I know only those I meet here every day.
Mama and Baba, I want to be proud of who I am.
But you have to show me all the things you
tell me about.
So take me back home. Show me my grandmother.
The one I remind you of.

Show me my uncles, my aunts, cousins, all my family.
Take me back so I can speak my language everyday.
So I can eat my food and learn to love it –
So I can sing our songs and dance our dances.
Let us go back home so we can sit under our tree
Warm ourselves by the fire and listen to the stories
about our ancestors.

Let us go back home to our country, to our family
Let us go back to where we belong.
But you say we cannot do that.
We can't go back home
Not now, not yet.
And when I ask why?
You tell me it is because we are Refugees.

Maybe, someday in the future, I will see all the
things my parents talk about, and share in their
memories.
"Some day we shall go back home."
So they tell me.

Mama – let me tell you something
I don't want to be a Refugee all my life.

Elsa Tesfaye Musa
Eritrean refugee in Kenya, 1984

A mother's reflection about
a conversation with her
daughter

WHAT IS A REFUGEE?

What is a refugee ?
Well and good to answer.
To answer such a question
we need to be careful,
because those who can answer it are very rare in this world.

To answer such a question,
needs you first to take refuge,
otherwise your answer will be simple and meaningless.

As refugees,
we are victims of violence and war.
We left our motherland
because we were being mistreated in many ways.
We ran to get protection in other countries.

But as a refugee,
you are always simple in front of anybody.
You are subject to prejudice and mistaken always.
You are a human being without any value.
You can pass through any disaster
and nobody will care about you.

Oh! What is lovely like our homeland?
In your own country, you are free,
free like a butterfly when it flies from flower to flower,
free like a fish moving in the water.
Homeland is a second heaven.
Without your home
you are like a dog without a tail.

Give us peace,
to return back to our beloved country,
our previous heaven Sudan.
Give us our ancestors' land.
Africa, live in peace forever!

ANDREW MAYAK
*Sudanese refugee in Kakumo
refugee camp, Kenya*

*reprinted from
Tilting Cages: An Anthology of
Refugee Writings, edited and
published by Naomi Flutter and
Carl Solomon, Sydney, Australia,
pp.10,11*

COLOURBLIND

Born pink,
grew-up chocolate brown
and was seen as coloured.
Some I hear are born pink,
grow up white, blush pink
and even with an acquired tan
never become coloured –
they live and die white.
But the blood that courses through all
is bloody, bloody red.

Born pink,
grew-up chocolate brown
and lived with the fear of spreading
the colour disease with a touch.
Those who shrank and shuddered to touch
Went constantly, seeking the Sun
to add colour and change the white!

Born pink,
grew-up chocolate brown
I live with the fear of hearing the four-letter word,
spelt P-A-K-I, spat at me.
We are asked to walk that extra mile,
show that third cheek to be slapped,
and have nineteen hundred lives,
so that we can revive after each fatal blow.

Born pink,
grew-up chocolate brown
our egos are punctured,
and our self-esteem severely ruptured
Whole but handicapped,
mute and silenced we watch
our children born pink,
growing up chocolate brown
with that blood that courses through all
still bloody, bloody red.

SUDHARSHANA COOMARASAMY
July 1990
*Sudharshana Coomarasamy fled
from Sri Lanka in 1984 with her 8-
month old twins and was a church-
sponsored refugee in Canada in
1986. She is an active advocate of
the rights of refugee and immigrant
women.*

*reprinted from Intricate
Countries: Women Poets from
Earth to Sky, published by Artemis
Enterprises, RR#2, Box 54,
Dundas, Ontario, Canada L9H
5E2 – Artemis@icom.ca*

Das kleine Dorf

Das Glockengeläut der Kirche
die Zeit erinnert mich.
Ich bin hinter dem Fenster,
und meine Einsamkeit,
und meine unendlichen Nächte.
Auf der anderen Seite des Fensters
lachen die Leute, sind glücklich
und glauben mir nicht.
Ich höre das Glockengeläut.
Der Morgen kommt
Ich schrei nach Liebe.

Bad Berneck, 7. Juli 1996

Ich muss die gläserne Nacht brechen
und rufe meine Geduld.
Ich muss das Fenster der Fremde
aufmachen und lasse meine
Einsamkeit fliegen
Ich muss bleiben,
singen
und sage dem Schmetterling:
"Das ist mein Morgen,
spiele glücklich und froh."

Bad Berneck, 2. September 1996

BEHROZ NAYEB GHANGER HOSSINI
iranischer Asylbewerber, lebt seit Sommer
1995 in der Nähe von Bayreuth, Deutschland

Church Bells

In the village
the church bell chimes
the hour calls me back.
I am behind the window
with my loneliness,
with my endless nights.
Beyond the window
people laugh and are happy
and do not believe me.
I hear the sound of the bells,
Morning is near
I cry out for love.

Bad Berneck, 7 July 1996

I must break through the glassy night
and summon up my patience.
I must throw wide the alien window
and let my loneliness fly free.
I must stay
I must sing
and to the butterfly say,
"Here is my tomorrow,
be joyful, be happy and play."

Bad Berneck, 2 September 1996

BEHROZ NAYEB GHANGER HOSSINI
Iranian asylum-seeker, living in Bayreuth,
Germany

(translated by the WCC Language Service)

Children's Rehabilitation Centre, Quezon City, Philippines (1990)

I always remember when my family used to live together until my father left and later my mother was imprisoned.

DAN

A 15-year old boy who was separated from his parents due to militarization. His mother was detained and his father had to leave home permanently because of constant threat and surveillance from the military. The Children's Rehabilitation Centre, where Dan did this drawing, assists children in developing the capacity to adapt and cope with socio-emotional and psychological problems due to military violence.

DEUTSCH ODER?

Wer sind sie? –
Ich bin Deutscher
Sprechen Sie deutsch? –
Nein.
Singen sie deutsch? –
Nein.
Lesen Sie deutsch? –
Nein.
Verstehen Sie mich auf deutsch? –
Ja, ein bisschen, aber lieber
spreche ich russisch.
Singen Sie russisch? –
Sehr gern.
Essen Sie gern "Pelmeni"? –
Oh, prima.
Kennen Sie die deutsche Küche?–
Ja, einiges kochen wir schon,
aber öfter "Borschtsch".
Kennen Sie Christa Wolf ? –
Wen?
Na und Goethe? –
Ja, schon mal in der Schule gehört.
Russische Dichter? –
Ja, viele gelesen.
Sie kommen aus Russland? –
Ja, bestimmt.
Wieviel Länder gibt es in der BRD? –
Gibt es hier jetzt auch
schon mehrere?
Gefällt Ihnen Dürers Stil,
Kleider zu malen? –
Nee, Kleider werden bei uns genäht.
Die "Zauberflöte"? –
Noch nie geblasen.

YOU'RE GERMAN, AREN'T YOU?

Who are you?
I'm German
Do you speak German?
No
Do you sing in German?
No
Do you read in German?
No
Do you understand me in German?
Yes, a little, but I prefer
to speak Russian
Do you sing in Russian?
Often
Do you like "Pelmeni"?
I love them
Do you like German cooking?
Yes, some of it,
but more often we cook "Borschtsch".
Have you heard of Christa Wolf?
Who?
What about Goethe?
I heard the name at school.
Russian poets?
I've read lots.
You come from Russia?
Yes
How many states are there in
Germany?
You mean you have many
states here too now?
Do you like the way Dürer
paints clothes?
Not really, at home we sew clothes.
The Magic Flute?

Wo leben sie eigentlich? –
Na hier.
Wo hier? –
In Deutschland.
Schon lange? –
ach, zwei Tage.
Und Sie verstehen
mich auf deutsch? –
Ganz schlecht.
Lesen Sie deutsch? –
Ich buchstabiere.
Singen Sie deutsch? –
Lieber russisch.

Sprechen Sie deutsch?
Ob ich spreche?
Und wer sind Sie?
Wieso fragen Sie?
Klar, ein Deutscher.

I never played one
Where do you live anyway?
I live here.
Where, here?
In Germany
Have you been here long?
Just two days
And do you understand me in
German?
Not very well
Can you read German?
I can make it out
Do you sing in German
Russian is better

Can you speak German?
Can I speak it?
So who are you?
Why do you ask?
I'm German, of course.

ILSA TICHONOVA
Lebt seit September 1996 in Deutschland. Sie ist deutschstämmige Kirgisin (veröffentlicht in der "Zeitung der Deutschen Kyrgystans", Oktober 1994)

ILSA TICHONOVA
Ilsa Tichonova has been living in Germany since 1996. She is a Kirghiz of ethnic German origin (reprinted from "Zeitung des Deutschen Kyrgystans", October 1994)

(translated by the WCC Language Service)

We Have Come to Know
the Solution to Our Problem !

We are refugees from Eelam
We have taken refuge in India.
The Organization for Eelam Refugees Rehabilitation
has provided us with various trainings
One of them is training in Leadership and
It is in this training that we understood
    ourselves and others
We learnt that our lives should have
    important goals.
The message gave us a small story, to illustrate
How wrong interpretation and communication
    led us astray.
We have reached a stage fit for leadership.
We have learned to obey
We have also learned to lead
We have also studied and known
Best qualities of leadership.
Problems crop up amongst us.
We did not know how these problems arose,
    and we did not know how to solve them
But, now we are clear about solutions
    after the training.
Now we know the basic reasons why problems arise
We have also learned to find solutions
What is important is service not the mere show

All these we learned after our training
These trainings provide different arts
Various tactics are employed to
    Inculcate the essentials
Dramas are also acted to bring out the
    meanings clearly
Lectures and speeches are taken.
Recourse to all these methods
    encouraged us still more.

T. THAVARAJINI

Came as a refugee from Jaffna, Sri Lanka, to Tamil Nadu, India, with her mother and brother and lives in Thappathy camp for refugees. Later, when her mother had gone to Saudi Arabia as a housemaid, she was entrusted with the responsibility of caring for her brother. This responsibility prevented her from going beyond the 10th grade. This did not stop her from serving the community. During her free time she serves as a nursery teacher and helps the women's group in the camps, motivating young girls in their education. She also participates in the campaign against women leaving their children and going to Saudi Arabia as house maids (translated by Organization for Eelam Refugee Rehabilitation (OfERR).

Programme of Jesuit Refugee Service, Cambodia

SOKHUEM

Watercolour. Sokhuem is a Cambodian child victim of a landmine explosion.

CHAPTER TWO
TESTIFYING TO OPPRESSION

STORMY SEAS WE HAVE BRAVED

Stormy seas we have braved and come
Having roamed and strayed as refugees we have come
Torn from near and dear ones we have come
Pleading for our rights we have come
It is the truth of the matter
Indeed the burden of our problems
Still awaiting the dawn

Having lost our homeland we have come
Scattered and lost one by one we have come
Having guarded our self-respect we have come
In fear of death and destruction we have come
It is the truth of the matter
Indeed the burden of our problem
Still awaiting the dawn

Thousands of dreams have we dreamed
Have seen them all being shattered
To the bosom of our mother we have come
With hunger and ill health we are buffeted
It is the truth of the matter
Indeed the burden of our problems
Still awaiting the dawn

EELATHU RATNAM

This song, composed in Tamil and translated by Sam Coilpillai, describes how refugees crossed the sea from Sri Lanka to Tamil Nadu, India, in 1992. After completing his secondary education Eelathu Ratnam moved to the capital city of Colombo and began to direct stage plays. Thereafter he produced Tamil and Sinhala films. In 1983 he had to flee his country with his family to Tamil Nadu, India, where he joined, as a volunteer, the Organization of Eelam Refugee Rehabilitation (OfERR). He composed many songs which brought out the innermost feelings of the refugees. In 1994 he met with a tragic accident whilst travelling (in India) on his two-wheel vehicle and died as a result. The refugees at the camp have continued to use song and poetry to express themselves.

UNTITLED

HASSANLI BERUZ
Armenian asylum-seeker in Bamberg, Germany

Exiled by the Storm

I

Prakerine[1], how can I send these words,
through the brown of your photo,
through salt air, through hot damp wind
through high trees, to the point
where you sit, holding your spirit, still
in hour hands, and perhaps, holding mine.
Are you asking the question,
what place am I in,
and what was the journey?

Here are my words.
I write them for Laos, and for you.

II

Once, Laos, you were
both kingdom and king.
Your rivers flowed smoothly, in the market
our words ran free like rice
spilling out from full baskets.
And always the sun
lay on the water
and there was a stillness
in the heart of the lake.

But now the world has spun round
like a wheel, casting your fate.
A wave of the sea has caught you,
has tossed you up high,
and will throw you down,
break you, and break you again.
You've become like the lotus
whose faint petals turn into steel
are ground to machines.

Now I remember
The sound of the sword
slicing the head from the neck.
Now I remember the sight of the head

1) Female name or used to
refer to a young woman

falling, the blood running.
I remember that hearing, that seeing,
and my spirit leaving my flesh.

And not only I, but all of my people
heard that same sword, saw the same blood
and fear leapt at them,
caught them like a ghost.
They could not speak, not move,
their spirits were gone,
their bodies were hard as stone.

Each has been cut from the other,
teacher from student,
girl from her lover,
husband from wife,
child from mother,
all have been ripped from their homeland.
Their hearts are burnt black by the fire,
tears crack on their faces.

Suddenly anger tears through me.
My enemy's face, the face of the beast,
is before me. I want to go back,
grab the gun, and kill the hyena.
I want to brandish the knife,
slice through the heart of its heart
and pour in the salt.
For there is no justice in him.

III

At midnight, the Mekong River
is needles of ice.
When you swim,
it will turn you this way,
or that way, or spin you around.

Suddenly there's a soldier shooting.
The bullets are like the monsoon
on the water behind you.
Then you catch a small cry,
Help me, my friend.
There's no chance. You can't help,
it's too late. The current is strong,
it's dragging your body away.

You can't reach him.
You fall through the water,
push up, fall again,
one day, if the wind swings about,
and the river pours in
through your mouth.

Oh Mekong, once you were friend
and in you, the Lao and the Thai people
danced, for New Year.
But now you have changed.
The open palm of your hand
has become the hard back of your fist.

IV

Prakerine, look at me.
Now there are ten years between us.
Have you walked to the temple for marriage?
Is there a man you have loved?
To me, it is just yesterday
that you and I planted the rice
in the field together, not caring
for rain, for the cold,
for the pain in the back,
not fearing the dangerous shadows,
because we stood close, you and I.

Now I am alone, with no home,
no homeland, no friend,
my words are worth nothing,
and only your photo, to bring me
that world, and that kingdom.
One day, if the wheel turns over,
completes the wide circle,
one day if the wind swings about,
blows in the new season,
I will come back
to Vientiane, and to you.

SANEHA LAUKAPHONE
A Lao poet (published in Lao with English translation in Refugee and Resettlement and Wellbeing, Mental Health Foundation of New Zealand, 1989, pp.49-51)

IT HAPPENED... ONE MORNING...

One morning... the sky was hidden
    behind the clouds
    Policemen came
    They woke up my mother
    Interrogating her about me and
    my companions.

Another morning...
    They came back, again
    They went in my room
    They set fire in my papers
    And they rummaged my books
    They terrorized my brothers.

Another morning...
    When dawn was smiling
    And the birds in the forest were singing
    I bade farewell to the village
    And my family
    Clinging to my passport
    And I fled far away...
    With a heavy heart.

حدث ذات ذات صباح...

شعر: عامر اليعقوبي

- تونس -

ذات صباح ... والسماء معتمة
قدم العسس
أيقظوا أمي
سألوا كينراعني وعن
رفقتي

٭ ٭ ٭

ذات صباح آخر
عاد الحرس
دخلوا غرفتي
أحرقوا ورقي
بعثروا كتبي
أفزعوا إخوتي

٭ ٭ ٭

ذات صباح آخر...
والفجر ضحوك
وعصافير الغابة تنشدو
ودعت القرية والأهل
وحضنت جواز السفر
وارتحلت ...
مرة رحلتي
/

- روما خريف 1993 -

YACOUBI AMEUR

Rome, autumn 1993

Born in Kairouan, Tunisia, migrant in Italy

Ecumenical Humanitarian Service, Novi Sad, Federal Republic of Yugoslavia

SACRIFICE

PERO MANDIÉ

Refugee from Sanski Most, Bosnia, born in 1938. He was a well known painter before the war. This painting is part of a series entitled "The world that is gone away."

I still remember when I was six years old. My father was building a cave. It was a very strong cave and a huge cave. If it was hit by a bomb, the bomb wouldn't go through it. When there was a fight everybody would run into our cave.

One day three planes were flying over the mountains. They were flying for two days. Everybody was afraid to come outside. They were afraid the planes would shoot at them and they would get killed.

The third day everybody came out of their houses because the planes didn't throw bombs or missiles. I was really happy. I went outside and played tackle with my cousin Kovan and some of my friends. And then I saw those planes turning around and heading straight to our village. Me and my cousin didn't have time to run into my father's cave. The planes opened fire at the houses and the people. I saw a cat running to the same cave me and my cousin were running to. It was hit by a shell. Me and Kovan ran into a dirty and dark and little cave that was filled with two feet of water. My father was looking for me, but he couldn't find us. I was so scared. I was shaking like I was under the ice and freezing to death. I couldn't cry. Two girls ran into the same cave I was in. They were wearing red dresses. The soldiers in the plane saw them. They threw bombs at us. The cave was hit by a bomb. Three people died in front of me and one behind me. One of my friends got shot on his shoulder by a piece of bomb. It hit one side of his shoulder and came out of the other side. He didn't feel anything. Blood was all over him.

The planes left. I got out of the cave and I saw the cat cut in half. I looked up. I saw smoke and broken houses, and then I saw my mother crying and saying, "My son is dying". I looked at my hand. I saw blood. I cried more. I had no idea I was shot. I didn't feel anything. That day sixteen people got shot and four died. There was only one doctor in my village. He gave me some medicine. The other people needed doctors immediately. There was only one tractor in the village. There wasn't room for me to get on.

That changed my life not to be afraid of sounds and blood and many things.

Diyar Amin

Diyar Amin, aged 15, is a refugee from Kurdistan who has been in the US since 1993. The story was written in October 1996 as an assignment at the English as a Second Language (ESL) class. Students were asked to write about an incident that occurred in their past that changed their lives in some significant way.

PRISON

I, the Lord... will make you to
be a covenant for the
people... To open the eyes
that are blind, to free captives
from prison...
(Isaiah 42:6,7, NIV)

NONO O. PARDALIS
*Pasyal-pasyal at iba pang
paglalakbay, Philippine High
School for the Arts, 1997
(translated by Diwata Hunziker).
Nono came to the Children's
Rehabilitation Centre, Quezon
City, Philippines, when he was 9
years old in 1987. His mother was
a political prisoner and his father
was an organizer of unions during
the Akino administration and
became a missing person. Nono
later attended the National School
of Arts where he also became a
student leader. The Children's
Rehabilitation Centre assists
children to develop the capacity to
adapt and cope with socio-
emotional and psychological
problems due to military violence.*

as the teeth of the truncheon rips my thigh
and a thousand blows rain on my head —
in prison was I thrown
      where even the wind cannot escape
      where rats and cockroaches cannot talk;
      and the guard is the god of
      guns and bullets.

the food cannot nourish me
neither water nor coffee can quench my thirst
dreams have ceased
in prison that even the sunlight cannot reach.

dark.
blinding darkness.
i can't see, i can't feel
the desire to be free.
dark.
blinding darkness.
i can't see, i can't feel
even my principles.

the searing pain hits my thigh
slashing my heart
slashing my conscience
repeatedly ripped by the truncheon
and the darkness.

scars do not heal here
where time knows no bounds
where there is no sun, moon
or stars.

i will be thankful
the moment time comes
      and my final breath sets me free.

Ecumenical Refugee Programme, Athens, Greece

TORTURED

SCULPTURE BY SIRWAN SAID SOFY
32 year-old Kurdish refugee from Iraq in Greece

The Executions

Bored as I was, I began, along with a few other inmates, to make worry beads. The dough of the bread was the material we used to form the beads, and we used powdered paint to colour them.

At this time prisoners were being regularly taken for interrogation. They usually wore oversized slippers to these ordeals. The reason for this was that they were regularly whipped on their feet, and in consequence the feet would swell. Had they not taken their oversized slippers, they would have had to walk back to the cell on bare bruised feet.

The daily departure of these prisoners to the prosecutor's office created an incredible atmosphere of terror in the cell. I continued to make worry beads and observe my cellmates. The number of prisoners had drastically increased.

The number of prisoners beaten was also on the rise. I remember well Shahin, a dark-faced girl. She belonged to one of the leftist groups. I asked her to show me her bruises. She laughed and said that because of her dark skin, the bruises could not be seen. I followed each case with avid curiosity. It seemed in some cases that the whole body was one big bruise.

The next night I saw Shahin in the bathroom again. She seemed happy as she chatted to her friend — apparently she had gone to another interrogation, and now felt that the danger had passed. A couple of days later, she seemed rather nervous again: and that night she was summoned once more to the prosecutor's office. The next day, her name appeared on the list of those who had been executed. I had by then become a friend of her friend and I asked her about Shahin. Apparently, Shahin's crime was to have been the driver of a car in the trunk of which a small printing press had been hidden. On the last day of her life, Shahin had told her friend that she thought she was going to be executed. She knew this because the interrogator had fondled her breasts, and that was a sure sign of doom.

The truth is I have never seen a political prisoner who had been sexually abused or molested. There was a rumour that virgins condemned to die were married to the Revolutionary Guards before their execution. According to tradition, if a virgin girl is buried, she will take a man with her. Since no one who was executed ever came back to speak of their experience, I was never able to verify this rumour. Shahin's words are my only proof. I also know of a couple of prisoners who came very close to having sexual relations with their interrogators. In one case the cause was the girl's clever attempt to avoid torture. The second case was a heated love affair between a prisoner and her interrogator.

Toward the end of September, the number of prisoners who could not walk was on the increase. They had been badly whipped on the soles of their feet. After a while a swollen lump, the size of an orange, would appear on the bottom of their feet. One of the biggest problems for these prisoners was walking to the bathroom. Some found a clever solution: they turned a big metal container of cheese into a chamber pot. They installed a thin layer of foam around the rim of the pot; three people would embrace the wounded prisoner and gingerly lower her onto it.

One night, as we lay in the dark, I decided to go to the bathroom hoping to avoid the long line in the morning. It was one o'clock in the morning. Prisoners were lined up next to each other on the floor. They were all awake. There was absolute silence in the cell. Something ominous was in the atmosphere. There was no line for the toilet. Instead, a few prisoners stood around and took turns to climb up on the water-heater and look out. When I approached, I saw one of the girls trembling. Although we were not friends, she held my arm and quietly said that the bodies of prisoners were being lined up in the yard. From about eleven o'clock that night, a piercing sound had been heard at more or less regular intervals. One of the prisoners suggested that the authorities were constructing a new visiting centre and what we heard was the sound of steel being unloaded. The girl I was with became visibly more shaken when the sound was heard again. I asked her about the sound. She said it was machine-gun fire.

By the time that long and bitter night finally passed we had counted more than two hundred and fifty "coups de grâce". In the newspapers the next day, I found the names of more than three hundred people who had been executed.

The following day was even more awful for everyone in the block. They took a few prisoners from each block to the office of the prosecutor. There, after summary trials lasting between two and five minutes, the prisoners were divided into two lines. One line was taken to be executed, the other was returned to the cells. The intent was probably to bring terror to everyone. Many of the prisoners who were called to trial that night behaved abnormally for many months afterwards. I saw one of them occasionally fall as she walked, and then get up and continue as though nothing had happened. Another sat the whole night gazing at the toothbrushes, the towels, and the jackets of the executed prisoners...

That same day, they brought Holou to our block. She was a shy girl and stood in a corner motionless. I asked her her name. "Holou", she replied. It was a habit of the Mujahadin to give a false name at the time of arrest. In prison, they would call one another by names of flowers, fruits, and animals. The leftists also had the same habit. Holou, Persian for peach, truly resembled her name.

I told Holou that I would like to know her real name. With tears in her eyes, she said she had already died four times. She explained how from the moment of her arrest up until our conversation, the guards had simulated her execution four times. Twice the Revolutionary Guards had stormed a bus ferrying prisoners, pretending to go on a rampage. On another occasion, they had stood her against a wall, told her she was going to be shot, and then fired blanks at her. I forget the details of the fourth experience. As we talked, it was clear that something had truly died in her: she was only fifteen years old and I was filled with silent rage about her torments.

Another of the prisoners, named Golshan, seemed deeply melancholic. I was told that only last week her father, along with other monarchists, had been executed. I tried to help this young girl and soon became friends with her. Before her incarceration, she had performed her prayers religiously, but then quit them upon her arrest. She had been at an engineering college somewhere in England; around Easter time she had returned to Iran to marry her fiancé. Her father was a member of a monarchist group and as bad luck would have it, when Revolutionary Guards raided her father's office to arrest him and other members of the group, she was in the office. As she claimed, and I have no reason to doubt it, her only participation in the group was typing one of their letters. She was arrested along with everybody else. During interrogation she had behaved badly, being utterly intransigent on matters of rather dubious significance. For instance, she had refused to wear a veil or to remove her nail polish from her fingers. The sight of her father's execution changed her radically. I think she tried to compensate for her father's timorous behaviour during his trial by her own valour.

While in Evin prison, she had a dream that she related to me. She dreamt that she was engulfed inside an octopus. A big tendril forcefully entered the entrails and plucked someone from inside each organ, placing them in another tendril. Golshan began to scream, "Take me too! Take me too!" and she ran after the big tendril. The tendril deposited the abducted people on top of a hill and Golshan heard the voice of the Octopus saying, "I just had this hankering to bring them out here."

The dream was important. In prison, the killing grounds were called "hills". In hindsight, I regret I did not try at the time to analyze her dream for her. I only told her, "Golshan, be careful." As was her habit, she took some pills and hid under a blanket. Under the blanket was her only place of solace.

Towards the end of November, overcrowding in the prison reached an explosive point. There were more than three hundred and fifty people crammed in our few cells. Every night, a group of prisoners were forced to stand in a corner, because there was not enough room for everyone to sit down. Summary trials and mass executions had become routine... I was tired and disheartened. I felt the weight of all the corpses on my shoulders. In one way, though, I felt happy to be in prison in these treacherous times; I knew that if I were free, and did not take any steps to protest the executions, I would have forever hated myself. But the unfolding catastrophe was much bigger than anything I could do, bigger even than anything a political group could do. In captivity, one is not tormented with these problems, for there is definitely nothing one can do. I knew that when the sad history of these days came to be written down, then at least my role would be clear.

Albert Camus, in his interpretation of the Sisyphus myth — the man who had killed his son and was commanded by the gods to spend eternity pushing a rock up a steep hill so that it can roll down again — claims that the man was happy because he need make no choices. Now, in prison, in times of bloody and banal brutality, I too was happy because I need not make any choices. I had not asked to be in this position, but I made no efforts to escape from it, leaving my fate in the hands of the Hezbollah.

SHAHRNUSH PARSIPUR   *A prolific short storywriter and has published several novels. "The Executions", from unpublished memoirs, was translated from Farsi by Abbas Milani (reprinted from This Prison Where I Live: The PEN Anthology of Imprisoned Writers, ed. Siobhan Dowd, Cassell, Wellington House, 125 Strand, London WC2R OBB, and 127 West 24th Street,*

Iran, 1981   *New York, NY 10011, 1996)*

DECEPCIÓN

Nuestros hermanos llegaron
desde lugares lejanos
aparecieron llenos
de sed

Nos levantamos
y dimos de comer
el mejor carnero
atizamos en el fogón
sancochando en olla de barro
oca colorada

Cuando te extraviaste
en las punas solitarias
buscando el buen ichu
llore varios días
por no encontrar tu rastro

En el mal tiempo
retoceamos con tu quillango
en la pampa del cóndor
hasta el confín de las estrellas

te amé como a mi madre
durante el Santiago en tu nombre
chacché dulce a la madre coca,
bebí el trago amargo,
imploré al Dios Wamaní

Hoy,
me das la cara
y golpeas mis espaldas,
confundes nuestros principios y
creas pánico entre los hombres,
robas a tu hermano y
hasta a tu madre has herido,
que decepción

El autor es miembro de la Comunidad Cristiana de Desplazados, en el Perú Taller de Arte, 1996

DISAPPOINTMENT

Our brothers and sisters came to us
from distant places.
They arrived
parched with thirst.

We got up
and gave them food,
our best Lamb.
We stoked the stove
and cooked a red vegetable soup
in our earthenware pot.

When you got lost
on the lonely Andean high plateau,
looking for good icho grass,
I wept for days
because I could find no sign of you.

When the weather was bad,
we cuddled in your fur blanket
on the grassy highlands, where the condor flies,
near the edge of the world of the stars.

I loved you as my mother,
at the feast of St James,
I chewed the sweet leaves of mother coca bush.
I drank the bitter draught.
I pleaded with the god Wamaní.

Today,
you stare me in the face:
you strike me in the back,
you are betraying our principles,
you are sowing panic among people,
and robbing your brothers and sisters.
You have even hurt your mother.
What disappointment!

The author is a member of the Christian Community of Displaced Persons, at the Peruvian Art Workshop, 1996

(translated by the WCC Language Service)

My Rights Are Not Heard

For a long time I am in the dark
My rights are not heard
They say you are a foreigner
Follow our rules

Even if I am a woman and a foreigner in Greece
I also have a heart that can be wounded
Most of all I am also a human being who feels hurt
Don't step on my humanity and my rights

Wake up Greece where I am now staying
Look at our situation
We are women asking for justice
What we NEED are AMNESTY AND FREEDOM

Anonymous

Regularization and amnesty are the major demands of undocumented, irregular and migrant workers not only in Greece but also in other parts of Europe (reprinted from Kababayan, December 1995, p.12)

TESTIMONIO

Era una noche, la peor noche de mi vida, ya que esa noche perdí todo de lo que tenía: Casa, ganado, mis padres y me quedé con dos hermanitos menores:

Esa noche entraron un grupo de terroristas, más o menos 20 personas, encapuchados, con armas y me dió miedo. Pero al ingresar en la casa, y mi padre no pudo colaborar con ellos dándoles alojamiento y comida, los terroristas mataron a sangre fría a mi padre y al ver ésto mi padre deseaba ayudar cubriéndole con su cuerpo, ella también murió. Todo éste cuadro pude verlo, oirlo,... Luego esa noche nos sacaron a mí, a mis hermanos pequeños y quemaron la casa y se llevaron parte del ganado, mejor dicho, luego de matarlos, se llevaron la carne que les serviría para su camino.

Nos quedamos con mi tía, y ella nos trajo al Cusco para alojarnos, pero yo vivía cada día con ese pasado muy duro. Me perseguía constantemente tanto que cada noche no lograba dormir.

Gracias a Dios que el grupo de personas del Centro de la Familia en el Cusco que lograron hacerme el tratamiento y apoyo a mi persona como a mis hermanos.

Sin embargo, lo que me pasó nunca se borrará de mi mente quedará grabado. Pero ésta experiencia que pasó muchos niños y mujeres sufren refugiadas en sus casa en los Andes de Ayacucho, Apurímac, y se que anhelan una libertad total de sus pesadillas y de sus propias vidas del pasado.

ANGEL (SENDÓNIMO)
Es una de la chicas que les brindamos apoyo, en ese entonces tenía 12 años. Actualmente tiene 16 años y estudia para terminar su secundaria.
Centro de la Familia - EIRENE PERU

A Testimony

It was night, the worst night of my life, because that night I lost all
I had — home, cattle, my parents — and I was left with my two
little brothers.

That night a band of terrorists came in, about twenty of them,
hooded and armed. They terrified me when they came in. My
father refused to collaborate with them by giving them shelter and
food and so they killed him in cold blood. My mother, seeing this,
had tried to protect him with her own body, and she too died.
I saw and heard all of this...

Then that night they took me and my little brothers out of the
house and burned it down and took away some of the cattle; or
rather, after killing them, they took them as meat for their journey.

Then we stayed with my aunt, and she took us to Cuzco to live,
but every day I kept reliving those cruel past events. They hounded
me constantly, so that I could never sleep at night.

I thank God that the people at the Family Centre in Cuzco were
able to provide treatment and help for me and my brothers.

But what happened to me will never be erased from my mind. It
will remain engraved on my memory. But many women and
children are suffering the same fate as me. They have taken refuge
in their homes in the Andes of Ayacucho and Apurímac, and I
know that they are longing to be completely free from their
nightmares and their own past lives.

ANGEL (PSEUDONYM)
*One of the children being supported by the Eirene Family Centre. At the time of these
events she was 12 years old; she is now 16 and studying to complete her secondary
education.*

(translated by the WCC Language Service)

QUIERO LIBERTAD

Más hermoso que el Sol
en el Verano que espero
es la libertad que anhelo.

Más hermoso que las flores
en la primavera de los Andes
es la libertad que anhelo.

Más hermoso que la comida
y ayuda que me dan mis amigos
y personas de mucho amor,
pero la libertad es mi anhelo.

La libertad es lo más hermoso,
sin libertad yo moriría,
y aquí lo voy experimentando.

Por eso grito a voz en cuello
que deseo MI LIBERTAD del
lugar donde ahora estoy.

I WANT FREEDOM

More beautiful than the sun
that I hope for in summer
is the freedom that I long for.

More beautiful than the flowers
in the Andes in spring
is the freedom that I long for.

More beautiful than the food
and help given me by my friends
and loving people
is the freedom that I long for.

Freedom is the most beautiful thing there is.
Without freedom I would die,
and here I have found it.

So I am shouting at the top of my voice
from the place where I now am
that I want MY FREEDOM.

PALOMA (SENDÓNIMO)
*Niña que sufrió con la pérdida de sus padres
por causa de la violencia terrorista en Los
Andes del Perú. Estuvo siendo apoyada por
el Centre de la Familia — EIRENE PERU,
ahora ya tiene 15 años y trabaja y estudia en
el Cusco. Sigue siendo apoyada por el
proyecto Múltiple.*

PALOMA (PSEUDONYM)
*A young woman who suffered the loss of her
parents through violent terrorist action in
the Peruvian Andes. She was supported by
the Eirene Family Centre project, Peru, and
is now 15 years old and works and studies in
Cuzco. She continues to receive support
from the Multiple Project.*

(translated by the WCC Language Service)

Armed Future

Infants trained to become infantry,
weaned from the breast and
introduced to the bomb;
Out of the womb and into war,
holding guns with two way barrels,
killing and being killed,
maiming and being maimed.
Men, movement, visions of victory,
creating mirages of liberation
or the long-waited self-determination.
Fed and filled with patriotic passion
unhesitantly exterminating elements,
fighting and dying for a cause —
superseding all other bonding.
Forced conscription claiming not only men & women
but also our should-be blooming children.
Mothers we are, rended barren,
robbed of motherhood, stilled and sterile.

Yet, theorists theorize
that our future is in the hands —
in the hands that now hold
AK-47's, RPG-7's and M-16's.
What if the hands that hold the future
are blown to smithereens
and are stilled to silence,
and our future dies in infancy —
at the hands of infants in infantry.

Sudharshana Coomarasamy

She fled Sri Lanka in 1984 with her 8-month old twins and was a church-sponsored refugee in Canada 1986. She is an active advocate for the rights of refugee and immigrant women. The United Nations has estimated that there are 250,000 children under the age of 15, bearing arms around the world today.

June 1990

Fadi Nawfal, Beirut, Lebanon

Untitled

Rita Chamooun

The drawing represents people dying in the war with the red rose being
watered by the blood of the dead.

8-year old refugee from Iraq. Her family sought refuge in Lebanon after the Gulf war.
The drawing was done in a refugee children's drawing class 1994. The instructors were
Iraqi refugees who were artists in their country. This programme was organized by the
Middle East Council of Churches' Service to Refugees, Displaced and Migrants (SRDM)

Yellow Ribbons

From Ninja Turtles to Nintendos
then proceeding to war in the Gulf.
We count the losses,
and mark the scores.
Men, women and children turned —
turned against each other;
turned towards alienation.
Losing tolerance losing hope,
in losing life and willingness to listen.
Listen in silence
to the noise of war.
Listen to each other
crying in despair.
Silent majority we've become
silently we condone;
Preparing to play another game,
unwittingly increasing our shame.
Denying humanity, safeguarding "democracy",
Who's to unmask the hypocrisy?
Schools, workplace and our home
go on with daily life and needs
careful to maintain the silence
all tied up neatly with yellow ribbons.

SUDHARSHANA COOMARASAMY

Scarborough, Canada
20 February 1991

Sudharshana Coomarasamy fled from Sri Lanka in 1984 with her 8-month old twins and was a church-sponsored refugee in Canada in 1986. She is an active advocate of the rights of refugee and immigrant women. In Toronto yellow ribbons welcomed soldiers back from Gulf war.

Afternoon Bombing

Skotinos George
A 59-year old refugee from Cyprus. The art work was created between 1974 and 1975.

What Is the Meaning of War ?

What is the meaning of war?
    war means hunger
    war means death
That is the meaning of war!

What is the meaning of war?
    war means killed men
    war means sad men
That is the meaning of war!

What is the meaning of war?
    war means blood
    war means tears
That is the meaning of war!

What is the meaning of war?
    war means horror
    war means terror
That is the meaning of war!

What is the meaning of war?
    war means deserted lands
    war means asking hands
That is the meaning of war.

Alejandro Figuerado   *A refugee from Cuba in the USA. This poem was written in the English-as-a-Second-Language class he attended.*

SALWA IBRAHIM SAWALHA

15-year old Palestinian girl, native of Yerba, in Rafah refugee camp. This is one in a series of 19 paintings she did on the theme of the Intefada.

She describes the painting: "We are left with nothing. Our vocabulary is full of words: demolition, detention, beatings, killings and closures."

DAS ÜBEL

EVIL

Ausserhalb des Verstandes
Weit weg von Gott
in der menschlichen Finsternis
Lebt
Das Übel

Beyond understanding
Far away from God
in human darkness
evil lives

KINDER IM KRIEG

CHILDREN IN WAR

Wessen Seele hört
Den Schrei
In welchen Fluss fliessen
Die kindlichen
Tränen ?

Whose soul hears
their scream?
Where is the river
that flows
with the tears of children?

PALIC DERVIS
*ist bosnischer Kriegsflüchtling mit
dem Status einer Duldung in
Deutschland.*

PALIC DERVIS
*A 29-year old Bosnian refugee with
temporary status in Germany*

*(translated by the WCC
Language Service)*

BOSNISCHE GRÄBER

BOSNIAN GRAVES

Aus dem
Westzimmer
Aus dem
Ostzimmer
Aus dem Herzen, mein Freund
Mit dem Gebet für die Toten
Bosnische Gräber
Spende

From the
West
From the
East
From the heart, my friend
With the prayer for the dead
Bosnian graves
Reach out

CHAPTER THREE
SEEKING THE RIGHT TO REFUGE

Portrait of a Nurse in a Foreign Country

Hard times
bind her throat
that she has to swallow
the choice
of the Damocles sword.

Papers incarcerate
her right
to cry
over her
chained wings.

The flame
on her Aladdin lamp
burns with care
for the sick
and for her
sick
self.

A nightingale
languid from labour
drained out of her wits
grounded by her own needs.

Seeking refuge
in a strange country
only to find out
that it's no shelter
but the waiting
vultures, serpents
and wolves
to delight
In her
defencelessness.

MAE ROCA
Jeddah, July 1987

*(reprinted from T.N.T. trends, news and
tidbits, official newsletter of Kanlungan
Centre Foundation Centre for Migrant
Workers, Quezon City, Philippines)*

1. Hurry up the UNHCR staff are right ahead of us
2. Let us wait for daddy
3. They have burned our home
4. Hurry up so that you are listed
5. Hide the children
6. If the French were not here we would be dead
7. They have caught my parents
8. They missed us. They arrived at the protected zone
9. Sit on the ground. Have you fled? What have you seen?

DRAWING BY MUGIRABAHGA JEAN S. AMOUR

Refugee from Rwanda in Tanzania, 1996. In the primary 2B class at Keza III holding site.

On Trial without Charges

We hid behind bushes,
laboured with birth pangs inside trenches —
Stretched a meal for husband and children,
and filled our bellies with water.

We gathered our family
under one roof — a tree.
We witnessed loss of life and property
and shuddered and suffered daily.

Some decided to brace the seas,
some the relentless desert lands.
Separation — the price of survival
traditions were broken to stay alive.

When at borders, ports and camps
our hosts surveyed us with doubts and disbelief,
and sought proof of our pain and loss,
we suffered and shrunk a little more.

SUDHARSHANA COOMARASAMY
January 1990
Sudharshana Coomarasamy fled
Sri Lanka in 1984 with her 8-
month old twins and was a church-
sponsored refugee in Canada 1986.
She is an active advocate for the
rights of refugee and immigrant
women (reprinted from Intricate
Countries: Women Poets from Earth
to Sky, published by Artemis
Enterprises, RR#2, Box 54,
Dundas, Ontario, Canada L9H
5E2, Artemis@icom.ca)

Our journeys are not over yet
in asylum we are in exile.
In resettlement we are on trial
Our charges are not clear to us.

Is it a crime to want to stay alive,
to raise your family without war and fear.
Is it a crime to cross borders
and seek refuge in a neighbour's house?

"The little food we receive we have to share with the rats... even when they do not stop destroying the bags."

IT HURTS ME

Home away from home
I felt incomplete
Abandoned and broken
Bowed and uncertain
Like a helpless orphan
Unsettled
Frightened.

Relying on them
For a handful of beans
To relieve my hunger
Food but nothing to think ahead
For discarded shirts
That can't cover my naked body
And the nakedness within.
Waiting their decision on my affairs
As beggars cannot choose
Feeling small and powerless
IT HURTS ME.

When my dream is shattered
Like a broken mirror
Of going back home
Where I belong to, to see a day-light
That can lift me from the night.

But unsettled is me... desperate
Daydreaming in camps... being locked
For lack of world attention
Thrown and rejected
IT HURTS ME.

ZEMED LIBEN
*Ethiopian refugee in Kakumo
Refugee Camp, Kenya*

*(reprinted from Kanebu —
Kakuma News Bulletin, March-
April 1996, newsletter published in
Kakuma refugee camp, Turkana
District, Kenya)*

Christmas is coming and you are gone.

Our son is not here either.

Our daughter is with me pretending that she is not forlorn. When she is alone she carefully gathers her tears into the small velvet boxes not knowing what to do with them later. I secretly watch her and repeat the words of the prophet Isaiah: "Their children will be smashed into smithereens in front of their eyes, their houses will be plundered, their women dishonoured... "

Yet another refugee died here. They say he lived in a bowling room where people look like skittles. Forgive me for putting it like this, but you should have been there to see it — everyone was standing still like skittles, watching the silence in disbelief, waiting to be struck down. This one was weighted down with cares. His diagnosis was written in Latin. I do not know the word for sorrow in that language. Has it been written as well?

They found his grave somewhere in the deserted flat landscape. Far away, where the distance rips your sight.

Only, he wanted a place close to yours, where cypresses grow from the rocks, where crickets give their concerts from spring to autumn and the evening music of our bells carries our prayers and prayers of our ancestors to God. The concert halls in the nature of our native land are nowhere so resonant and perhaps this is why not even the dead want to disown the primeval performances of their homeland.

We had to give them and we had to leave...

It is winter 1993. Christmas is just about to arrive with snowflakes on a green horse. Holy tree is quietly crackling. Bells are ringing. We are guarded by the soldiers of the United Nations. Islam Grcki and Kasic are welcoming the God.

Then the shells start falling from the sky. Houses shake. Children howl in pain and fear. Women wail. Vehicles are lighted ominously in their rush through the wounded night. Holy oaks fly to the sky...

They murdered Christmas on our doorstep!

Our village became a place of evil and violence.

I am calling you like in a dream. We are jumping into our car. Our luggage is made of dreams only. Everything else remained in the village. Our dreams went back there. We never did.

God Almighty, why did you let this happen?

Children are full of delight here. They are buying Christmas trees, small colourful balls, pieces of motley paper and fabric. They are doing all to colour their joy.

Our joy was left hanging. It is swinging now in the wind like a discarded cloth. Banging against burnt windows. Stumbling over the ruins of distorted houses. Tracking the deserted homes. It is kneeling in front of the sacred world of the centuries. And calling us from the Land of No Return. In its wanders it never comes to us. Not even joy wants to be exiled.

But we are here.

Christmas is coming again here in the lowlands on a green horse and snowflakes.

Children will be delighted again.

Ours dread the holy trees flying into the sky.

They fear that Christmas may get murdered on their doorstep again.

Susan, the red-haired girl from our neighbourhood, was not afraid. She died suddenly dreaming of chocolate. Here, I got one from the Red Cross with a European label on it and I would love to give it to the red-haired girl.

She was a little shy at school and used to sit at the rear desk where the wind bangs the windows violently.

– Why are you sad, little girl? Why aren't you catching the wind like your friends? You could tie it up and fly it or take it by a string if you like.

– No one likes my red hair. I have no money to buy the blond one. My mum doesn't want to bear me new hair.

I drew her many red little girls, then, whose hair streamed in the wind and it looked like poppies setting the fields into fire. I was overwhelmed by the red. I made red smiles, red games, red balls and scarves until Susan started to like red.

In a red twilight Ljubica, her grandmother, and Petar, her grandfather, were killed for no reason in front of her house.

Their Christmas was murdered at their doorstep.

Women also screamed, children were falling swept away like blades of grass. Everything happened fast, not even the sky had time to weep.

I know that Susan dreamt of chocolate and I do not know what to do with the one that has a European label on it. I would gladly crush it under my feet on the asphalt of Novi Sad because Susan, the red-haired girl from my neighbourhood, is gone.

So are you. You remained wrapped in a dream and I cannot find you anymore. I can hardly think of a postman who would deliver you the letters. If I ask the wind, I would wait for the answer too long. I counted on the whisper of the sea, but in no way can I ride over there or build a boat to sail to you. Perhaps for this too, I am sad tonight.

Jovan Mlinar

Novi Sad, Federal Republic of
Yugoslavia, January 1996

Jovan Mlinar was born in 1940 in Islam Grcki, a village near Zadar in the Republic of Croatia. Islam Grcki was destroyed in the civil war in 1993 and he lost his house, property and job as a teacher of Serbian language and literature. He was exiled to Benkovac in Srpska Krajina where he organized a school for refugee children. A refugee himself, he taught in this school for two years. His second exile was to Yugoslavia. Together with thousands of other refugees he arrived in Novi Sad in August 1995 and has been living there and writing short stories about the exodus of his people ever since. This is one of a collection of stories, "Letters with no address", written in January 1996. The letters are addressed to his wife who died in the war, before his exile (original in Serbian, translated by Aleksandra Stojanovic)

The Day I Will Never Forget

Because of hope I still live.
Because of hope I can sing and dance.
It is because of hope that I laugh.
It is because of hope that I love.
But the day I will never forget
is the day I was born.

I'll never forget that day.
That day I was born I'll never forget,
for the hand that touched me was
so strong
that it nearly made me lame.
The light that I saw was
so bright
that I nearly became blind.
The sound I heard was
so loud
that I almost became deaf.
Surely, I will never forget that day.

That day I will never forget.
That day was the day I first felt sad.
It was the day I tasted hunger
It was the day
I needed everything,
everything I couldn't get.
Never will I forget that day.

It was the day
I felt lonely
and unprotected from the cruelty of the world.
It was the day I felt cheated.
That day was the day
I knew hatred.
That day was the day
my love vanished.
I will never, never forget that day.
But because of hope I still live.

Jimmy Bosco Oryema
*Refugee from Uganda in Kakumo
Refugee Camp, Kenya (reprinted
from Tilting Cages: Anthology of
Refugee Writings, edited and
published by Naomi Flutter and
Carl Solomon, Sydney, Australia,
pp.90,91)*

Love and Protection

1997

Oil painting by Tamerat Abebe
"The most important thing for a refugee is Love... they need love and protection... Love is a wonderful symbol of life, development and progress."

Born in 1968, Ethiopian refugee in Egypt. He graduated from the fine arts school in Addis Ababa, Ethiopia, in 1993. In Egypt he teaches art to other African refugees at St Andrews Church Arts and Crafts Programme. His works have been exhibited in Egypt where he has received several certificates of recognition at national and international events.

Fadi Nawfal, Beirut, Lebanon

UNTITLED

GINA EL RAMAI

*11-year old Lebanese displaced in the Choug region, Lebanon. She did this drawing in
1994 in a class where children were asked to draw on the theme of the family. The class
was taught by adult Iraqi artists who were in Lebanon as refugees – a programme
organized by the Middle East Council of Churches (MECC) Service to Refugees,
Displaced and Migrants (SRDM)*

Fear caught my mind and heart!
    My childhood...! Fear and run is the name of the game!
Our home... has never been like a home once!
    A single sound of Gunshot, like a whistle of a racing team
In different directions, we all run!
    Only to be re-united in a distant Bush!
My youngest sister, Poni, only Two... also accustomed to this fate!
    She has learnt not to cry in this kind of moments!
This could attract the Gunmen, so she knows!
    Back home dark smoke of burning grass Thatched Tukuls could be seen.
Presumably, all food stores burnt down! No more food in our Gugu!
    This is dry season attack, so they say!
Government gunmen, so is said!
    What they really wanted, could not get into my head!
So, my fate and fear are Real!

My father decided we cross, cross to a neighbouring Country.
    More families we met over there.
Running from the same fate!
    Grouped in a big village-like compound!
Relief workers gave food and medicines to all.
    So, we are all called refugees! our new name!
No more Gunshots at least. No more running!
    We all went to school. We learnt different languages.
We had clothes, books and porridge.
    Natives of that land were kind.
Our parents had a land to cultivate.
    They grew lots of food enough for all.
The land owners had a share too.
    So, there was hope in eyes of all.
No sooner had we completed the school year
    than Gunmen from our country attacked!
    Rain of bullets and fire, tore down everything!

Our Tukuls, Gugus and classrooms, everything!
    Commotion all over, people running to all directions.
So, still, my fate and fear are REAL!

    Fear caught my mind and heart... again!
I swore to have a gun some day, when I am grown a man!
    "This is a solution, why not?" I thought
I only fear to kill, but could shoot to scare the gunmen.
    Let tomorrow come, when I am grown big!
Hate came into me...! to kill the Government gunmen.
    "NO, I ought to scare them away... for killing is a sin"?
I would look for this man... called Government!
    Kill him and all his family, once and for all!
Like how he killed mine!
    Let me look for safety...! buy time, to grow a man!
Buy a gun and determine his destiny!
    Fate of this man, called Government, his fey is my desire!
We could then, all return home.
    Home that belongs to us all, where we all belong!
So, my fate and fear will be unreal.

DAVID HAJAR YOANE
Musician/poet, south Sudanese refugee in Amman, Jordan

I have been taken away from my country... I cry for my country

BASMA YOLDA, 1994
10-year old Iraqi refugee in Lebanon. She did this drawing in a programme for child refugees organized by the Middle East Council of Churches (MECC) Service to Refugees, Displaced and Migrants (SRDM). Adult artists from Iraq who were also refugees helped children express themselves through art.

9   "Mother, we are dying with hunger"
11 "They are taking whatever there is to eat"
12 The employees of the Red Cross
13 The truck that carries medicines

DRAWING BY BAZAMSANGA JOSEPH

Refugee from Rwanda in Tanzania in primary grade at Keza III holding site

An Unhappy Life

One day in rags you flee from home, for you are persecuted,
And then you run, you run, you run seeking a shelter,
With dry throat, empty stomach and torn body.
You reigned over empires
Now you must stay in mice lairs
Imprisoned with thousands and thousands of your fellow-men.
You fed well your beasts
Today you must die starving
You left your wealth and eat sand here.
Every day while sitting in a little corner, hands taken into the legs
You plunge your glance into a far sky,
And wondering how the future will be: there's darkness
everywhere.
The seasons are the same
Like nights and days.

The sun never arises and the moon never appears.
The bees make no honey.
This land is utterly rocky
Infected with venomous snakes and its birds do not sing.
Little by little the suffering increases, you don't know what to do.
Children and babies quietly die in their mothers' arms.
Your eyes become red and full of tears.
You make up your mind,
The other world to find,
And leave this one where the lambs devour the wolves.
You mourn over your men:
They were slaughtered somewhere.
You're alone, very sick and sorrowful.

Samaty Houndjogbe 1993   *32-year old refugee from Togo in Ghana*

FLIGHT
1993

IRINA PERCEVA

In the foreground is the Holy Family – as uprooted people. In the background is the house that was burned by right-wing radicals in May 1993. Five Turkish women died in the fire while they were asleep. Irina Perceva is an asylum-seeker from Russia in the territory of the parish of Vettweiß-Froitzheim, Germany. She, her husband and two daughters were expelled in 1994 and now live in Chechen.

WHY DON'T YOU GO BACK ?

Please don't ask me
"Why don't you back?"
Do you think I like staying?
For twelve grains of beans,
two weeks rations,
to stay without soap,
suffering malaria and typhoid,
here in the bush,
with wind, dust, blowing trumpet,
where nature is playing,
its ugliest games.
Do you think I like staying?
Seeking second-hand clothes,
if I could help myself
if I could re-build my homeland
Do you think I like staying?
Without my wife, husband, children,
my father, mother, sister, brother, family,
without feeling homesick.

Please don't ask me
"Why don't you back?"
Humans destroying each other.
Where human sense has lost its value,
war, tribal, religious conflicts,
destroy peace, democracy.
Where there is war,
where there is conflict,
where there is fear of persecution,
where there is no democracy,
where human rights are violated,
I can't go back.
I am destined to suffer,
in exile,

until, I go back
until my time comes.
Until then, I will stay.

Please don't ask me
"Why don't you back?"
I would if I could.
World humanitarian community:
understand that
it is not simple, nor easy,
avoiding past memory.
I can't remove from my mind,
my traditional culture,
my sentimental torture,
the folktales of childhood,
never old, never dead,
stamped in my mind.

I have normal feelings,
I suffer for dignity.
Please, don't kill my broken heart,
by asking me
"Why don't you go back?"
I will if I can.
I wouldn't stay a moment,
when the new dawn comes.

YILMA TAFERE

*Ethiopian refugee in Kakumo refugee camp, Kenya (reprinted
from Tilting Cages: Anthology of Refugee Writings, edited and
published by Naomi Flutter and Carl Solomon, Sydney,
Australia, pp.7-9)*

Botschaft Aus Der Abschiebehaft

Ich habe Angst
Angst, die Euch draussen fremd ist und hoffentlich fremd bleiben wird.
Die Angst lebt bei mir im Bauch, im Kopf, in den Füssen, in den Händen.
Meine Hände zittern
und sind nass und kalt wie die Hände meiner Grossmutter, ehe sie starb.

Die Angst verlässt mich nicht im Schlaf.
Ich kann sie mit niemandem teilen and niemandem mitteilen: denn die
Männer, mit denen ich die Zelle teile, sprechen eine andere Sprache.
Wir verstehen uns nicht.

Ich denke, dass jeder von uns annimmt, dem anderen gehe es besser. Er
kommt sicher aus einem Land, in dem das Leben gerechter oder freier oder
gebildeter oder auch nur wohlhabender ist, als es je im eigenen Land sein wird
oder war.

Wir beobachten uns argwöhnisch.
Wie spricht die Polizei mit meinem Nachbarn? Ist sie freundlicher zu ihm als
zu mir? Warum bekommt er jede Woche Besuch von Deutschen und ich noch
nie bisher?

Es ist nicht wahr, das gemeinsam empfundene Bedrohung Solidarität gebiert.
Sie gebiert Egoismus und Argwohn.
Sie gebiert Zweifel und Hass.
Die Bedrohung im Abschiebegefängnis gebiert Isolation.

In den ersten Wochen hatte ich noch Hoffnung.
Hoffnung, dass der Richter mir glaubt.
Hoffnung, dass die Behörden mich anhören.
Hoffnung, dass es jenseits der Gitterstäbe noch jemanden gibt, der sich mir
zuwendet.
Die Hoffnungen sind zerplatzt.
Der Hass ist zerplatzt.
Die Sehnsucht nach Freiheit ist verschwunden.
Geblieben ist die Angst vor den Polizisten und Sicherheitsbeamten
im Land meiner Geburt.
Mir aber wurde gesagt: Angst ist nicht asylrelevant.

Ihr da draussen baut Transparente und
Fahnen auf.
Ihr sagt, dass der Tag des Flüchtlings sei.
Ihr hört Reden, unterbrochen von Musik.
Ich bitte Euch: Schweigt und riecht die Angst, die durch diese Wände kriecht.

Message from a Detention Centre

I live with fear
fear that you out there don't know, and hopefully never will.
Fear lives in my belly, in my head, in my feet, in my hands. My
hands shake; they are clammy cold, like my grandmother's before
she died.

Fear never leaves me, not even in sleep.
I cannot share it with anyone, I cannot tell it to anyone; because
the men who share my cell speak a different language.
We cannot understand each other.

I think each of us believes the other is better off. He probably
comes from a country where life is fairer or freer, more civilized or
just less harsh than it ever was or will be in our own.

We watch one another suspiciously.
The police are speaking to my neighbour. Do they treat him better
than me? Why does he get a visit from German people every week,
when I never do?

It is not true that danger shared breeds solidarity. It breeds
selfishness and suspicion,
doubt and hatred.
In the detention centre it breeds isolation.

ANONYMOUS
Diktiert am 15. September 1994,
abgeschoben am 19. September 1994

ANONYMOUS
Dictated on 15 September 1994,
expelled on 19 September 1994

In the early weeks I still had hope.
Hope that the judge would believe me
Hope that the authorities would listen.
Hope that beyond the bars was someone who might care for me.
These hopes are shattered.
The hatred has evaporated.
The longing for freedom has vanished.
Leaving only the fear of the policemen and the security guards
in the land where I was born.
But, they told me, fear is not grounds for asylum.

Out there you carry your placards and your banners,
saying this is Refugee Day.
You listen to speeches, with breaks for music.
Be quiet, I beg you, and smell the fear that seeps from these walls.

Untitled
1997

Mae Da
*Refugee from Karen State, Burma, in Huay Ka Loke refugee camp inside Thailand,
between 12 and 18 years of age. The drawing was done "...a few weeks after the Burmese
military crossed into Thailand and burned the camp and all possessions to the ground."*

WHO WILL HELP !
WHO WILL COME TO OUR AID ?

Just because we were born as Eelam Tamils,
We are carrying a volcano in our chests
Just because we speak the Tamil language
We are suffering our headaches.
Our young women who were used to decent lives
And who looked forward to a bright future
Are now languishing under the burden of widowhood.
Our young men whose fathers and mothers
Had dreams of fruitful future for their sons
Are carrying guns; and daily
Many are losing their precious lives,
And the ordinary civilians,
Although they are not engaged in this war,
They are refugees in their own land
They are refugees in Tamil Nadu
And in various other parts of the world
They are persons with neither roots nor roofs.
Who shall wipe out our misery?
How shall our expectations be fulfilled?
Who shall come to our aid?
We are in search of a solution.

R. HELMALATHA-GANESHAN
1994

Refugee camp, Arcot. Organization of Eelam Refugees Rehabilitation (OfERR), Tamil Nadu, India. R. Helmalatha-Ganeshan, 19, is a refugee from Mannar, Sri Lanka. Her father is a farmer. At the refugee camp she is a coaching class teacher; she is single and educated up to grade 12. Her mother and two younger brothers live in the same camp. After completing grade 12 she could not continue her education due to financial difficulties. However with the persuasion of OfERR she is following a degree course at the Open University, England. At the same time she is conducting classes in the evenings for the refugee children (translated from Tamil by OfERR)

There's No Place Like Home

KAMPUCHEA,
Houses above the ground
Fruit trees surround each one.
Every season they produce fruit
Providing food and their beauty.
How I miss the scenery of my country.

The air was fresh, mixed with the fragrance of blossoms
The sun shone over the green vegetation and the colourful flowers
Everything seemed calm and peaceful
How happy I was.

At evening family met
Together young and old
Parents advised children to be good,
Kind to other people
We must respect the elderly
People were cheerful and friendly.

The world is moving, the time is running forward
The new one becomes old, the small becomes big
Everything has to change, so too, my homeland.
The darkness covered the light
The good became bad and evil
People no longer could live in their own land.

There was humiliation, torture, killing,
Depriving of food
And creation of diseases.

Friends became enemies
Some killed their own for power,
To live in a better condition
People live in fear

Hoping to wake up in the same place
Not lying dead somewhere in the jungle
Faith and trust were not to be found.

The Communist leaders took away possessions,
Status, and all had to dress in black
They took husbands away from wives
Brothers from sisters,
Children from parents
And said everything belonged to the State
Even our own bodies
LIBERTY and EQUALITY were their key concepts
But they practised a BUREAUCRATIC system.

Suffering and pain forced my family
To leave our country behind
To find freedom in another land
My dear sisters died from malnutrition and disease.

No land, no home, no place to go
Thai soldiers put us in the refugee camp
Our lives depended on the UNHCR and the Third Countries for
resettlement.

Here in New Zealand is freedom and peace
I should be happy, instead I am sad.
Dream of past experiences, and still live in nightmares
All over again.
I feel guilty enjoying the freedom
Knowing my family, friends are left behind
Still live in the dark.

The innocent always suffer
Struggling to survive from starvation
From war, which may never finish
War among our own people wanting to rule the land
Now the country has ended
In Viet Cong hands.

Yes, I am parted from my country
But my mind will always be
With my beloved country
Where I belong.
How I wish Kampuchea will be at peace again
Then I can return
to see where I was born.

In New Zealand people are kind, friendly, greet me with a smile.
Some do not understand
They stare and swear at me
Tell me to go back to where I come from.
What can I say?
I want to say
I do not want to invade your country,
Take away others' opportunities
It's not easy living in other people's land
Forced to learn a new language
Take up new responsibilities
As never before
In order to survive once more.

I wish people would understand
The difficulties trying to lead
A life in a different country.
Powerlessness, acting mute and dumb
Using hands and sweat
Instead of mental agility
Alienation, no recognition, no status,
Disapproval, hostility from others.

Depression, stress, anxiety
Loneliness, withdrawal are only a few problems
Khmer people face in a new society.

SIVLEANG UNG
*A Khmer poet (reprinted from
Refugee Resettlement and
Wellbeing Mental Health
Foundation of New Zealand, 1989,
pp.55-57)*

Building the Bridge of Love

We came to this land seeking refuge
But what remains is tears, tears in both our eyes
We are left with our lives only, nothing else
We are experiencing nothing else but suffering, unlimited
suffering.

(we came)

Plan was laid by a terrorist group
and our nightmare goes on without end and our future without a
guiding star
When will this terrifying phase end
We will care and build a bridge – a bridge of love.

(we came)

We ask those hearts that received us well showering us with love
Just let us know what sin the refugees have committed
We are not people without gratitude,
We are your children until we return to our land.

(we came)

We are all one people even though the sea separates us
We are all Tamils by language and culture
The storm that burst in between will pass away
That should not change our ties and our relationship,
The Eelam people will not sway to change their direction.

(we came)

EELATHU RATNAM

Eelathu Ratnam produced Tamil and Sinhala films. In 1983 he fled to Tamil Nadu, India, where he joined, as a volunteer, the Organization for Eelam Refugee Rehabilitation. He died in a tragic accident in 1994 while travelling in India on his two-wheeled vehicle. The refugees at the camp where he was have continued to use song and poetry to express themselves and in popular education activities (original in Tamil, translated into English by Organization for Eelam Refugees Rehabilitation OfERR).

The Destiny
1976

Issam Mohammad Hillis
Palestinian from Bersheva, born in 1955

NAM MO A DI DA PHAT
VENERABLE LORD BUDDHA

I have lost members of my family in the war.
   I have seen friends and relatives made into "Witch Badjelly's
   Boy-Girl Soup".
   I have fled my homeland of misery, death and darkness.
   I have experienced and witnessed thirst, starvation, piracy,
   murder, rape and cannibalism as well and denial and rejection
   by other human beings at sea.

I have languished aimlessly in a dirty camp for months and years.
   I have endured all those pains and suffering Oh Venerable
   Lord Buddha for two reasons.

Firstly, it is my religious and cultural belief that any misfortune
   that Befalls me is just and fair punishment for the bad deed I
   committed in my past lives and in earlier years of the present
   life.

Secondly, I hope for a better and brighter life and future of my
   children in a new land that will become my home and my
   country.

I am now in that land of Hope, Freedom and Equality:

But:

   — My formal qualifications and experiences, if recognized at
      all, do not provide me a job in my field of expertise.

   — My yellow skin, flat nose and dark hair bring me distrust.

   — My small command for the local language makes it difficult
      for me to mix with my fellow workers – but I work Oh Lord
      Buddha, I work long and hard to make ends meet and to
      ensure my children a brighter future.

— My children do not achieve at school because of the language barrier. As they seem to understand and speak English better, I have to rely on them to be my brain and my mouth. They learn and adopt the new culture, the new ways and customs and reject me and my beliefs, my culture and my roots.

— My elderly relatives feel they are being held under house arrest. They only go out and see other fellow country people if I can take them.

Oh Venerable Lord Buddha, I am so sad. I have lumps in my heart and in my throat. I can talk to nobody about my sorrows, my heartaches. My fellow refugees are busy with their lives and their own hopelessness. My close relatives are miles away. I do not have a monk nearby to listen to me and to reassure me that all this suffering has a meaning. I cannot go to Your house to pray and bring my offerings so You could assuage my path.

Where can I go?

Who can I turn to?

How much longer can I carry on?

Where do I get my strength and support?

Nam Mo A Di Da Phat.

KIM HOANG MACANN
A refugee from Vietnam. After the initial period of resettlement she has worked as a secondary school teacher in Christchurch and as an English as a second language lecturer at Christchurch College of Education (reprinted from Refugee Resettlement and Wellbeing, 1989, Mental Health Foundation of New Zealand, pp.47-48).

CHAPTER FOUR
CALLING FOR PEACE AND LOVE WITH JUSTICE

El Hambre Morirá

El pueblo errante
camina buscando refugios
Los pueblos hermanos
no comprenden nuestra angustia;
nuestros hijos son extraños,
hambriendos de pan siempre están.

El hambre morirá
cuando todos como hormigas
sembrando la papa
danzemos alegres

El hambre morirá
cuando la madre tierra
haga florecer el maíz colorado,
cuando la chirmoya endulce
el alma de los niños;
cuando todos soñemos
en una infinita chacra verde;
cuando todos nos aceptemos
y dialogando formemos
un jardín eterno.

El autor es miembro de la Comunidad Cristiana
de Desplazados, en el Perú Taller de Arte, 1996

Hunger Will Die

We, a wandering people,
journey on, looking for refuge.
Our fellow peoples
do not understand our anguish.
Our children are foreigners,
always hungry for bread.

Hunger will die,
when we all, industrious as ants,
planting potatoes,
shall dance for joy.

Hunger will die,
when the red maize shall flourish
on mother earth,
when the custard apples
will make the soul of our children sweet,
when we shall all dream
in a vast expanse of green farmland,
when we all accept one another,
and, conversing together,
become an everlasting garden.

The author is a member of the Christian Community of
Displaced Persons, at the Peruvian Art Workshop, 1996

(translated by the WCC Language Service)

Untitled

Painting by Song Sotheary, aged 29, displaced person under Pol Pot

In The Beginning...

Our mother, source of all life,
Hallowed be your sweet name.
May your kingdom of love prevail.
Your will to nurture and enrich
be done on earth, as in other planets
and in the heavens around it.
Give us each day our sustenance and
help us to sustain each other in love.
Give us strength to abstain from violence,
forgive our excesses and our acts without love.
We beg you never to deny
the security and the warmth of your womb,
like infants we seek and suckle sustenance
do not deny us your breasts.
Our navel, the eternal reminder of our origin,
remind us our pledge to respect all living things.
Yours is the kingdom of compassion
now and evermore.

Amen.

Sudharshana Coomarasamy

Sudharshana Coomarasamy fled from Sri Lanka in 1984 with her 8-month old twins and was a church-sponsored refugee in Canada in 1986. She is an active advocate for the rights of refugee and immigrant women (reprinted from Intricate Countries: Women Poets from Earth to Sky, published by Artemis Enterprises, RR#2, Box 54, Dundas, Ontario, Canada L9H 5E2, Artemis@icom.ca)

25 March 1992

THE LORD'S PRAYER
MATTHEW 6:9-13

OUR FATHER WHO ART IN HEAVEN
You are in Istanbul, in our flats and hotels, in Taksim and Beyoglu.
You are within us and with us and in our homes.
You are in Africa, Asia, Caribbean, the Middle East, Latin America, North
America, and the Pacific, in Yugoslavia and Russia.
You are with the hungry and dying children in Somalia.
Also in Liberia, Bosnia, Ethiopia, Sri Lanka, Kuwait and Iraq.

HALLOWED BE THY NAME
Hallowed in the memory of Paul of Tarsus, Martin Luther King, Jr, Bishop
Shanahan in Nigeria, Bishop Lumbuin of Uganda, Pastor Joseph Ayo Babalola.
In Nigeria, Dr Ida Scudder of India, Florence Nightingale, David Livingston of
Africa and our parents and grandparents who taught us our faith.
And hallowed in the lives of Desmond Tutu of South Africa, Billy Graham of
the US, Benson Idahosa of Nigeria and Mother Theresa of Calcutta.

THY KINGDOM COME
A kingdom without police harassment, accidents, soldiers, murder and crime.
A kingdom of freedom and justice.
A kingdom with no borders and only one language.
A kingdom with Christ prevailing and equal rights.
A kingdom with one family, one faith.
A kingdom with harmony between humans and nature.

THY WILL BE DONE ON EARTH AS IT IS IN HEAVEN
In a creation free from pollution – with clean air, clean water and safe food.
In our homes and in our lives.
With hope and faith in God's will that our world will be free of war, hunger and
poverty.

GIVE US THIS DAY OUR DAILY BREAD
The bread of compassion in word and deed.
The bread of protection from evil and injury and guidance in the way we go.
Give us the bread of goodness and prosperity to share with others to bring them

to Christ.
The bread of patience and endurance.
The bread of unity to make us one nation, one people, one destiny.

AND FORGIVE US OUR TRESPASSES AS WE FORGIVE THOSE
WHO TRESPASS AGAINST US
Forgive our selfishness and our greed.
Our unfaithfulness and pride.
That you will treat us as we treat others.
Helps us to forgive and give us the grace to forgive and let go.
Help us to fulfil our debts.

AND LEAD US NOT INTO TEMPTATION, BUT DELIVER US FROM EVIL
The temptation of self-righteousness.
Keep us away from the occasions of sin.
Keep us from false use of our tongues and from unnecessarily opening our
mouths or inappropriate silence.
Save us from the evils of starvation, war and all injustice.
And help us do good to our neighbour as we would have God do to us.

FOR THINE IS THE KINGDOM AND THE POWER AND THE GLORY
FOR EVER AND EVER, AMEN
A kingdom of the merciful. Where there is love not hate, peace not war.
A kingdom without pain, hunger or sorrow.
A kingdom where there is food without money.
A kingdom where no one would be unemployed.
A kingdom where every man and every woman lives in equality.
And where all creatures respect each other, living in harmony and life eternal.
A kingdom where God has the power and the control.
Where He has created us with the power to choose good.
Where thine is the glory, not ours, but thine.
For ever and ever, Amen.

A PARAPHRASED VERSION BY THE AFRICAN FELLOWSHIP OF UNION CHURCH,
ISTANBUL, TURKEY, 1993
*This is the result of the weekly Bible study/fellowship time of migrants, refugees from
Ghana, Nigeria, Uganda and others, at the interdenominational Union Church which
meets in the chapel of the Netherlands consulate in Istanbul, Turkey.*

PEACE

Painted on a greeting card

TASHI TSERING
28-year old refugee, from Tibet in Dharamsala, North India; apprentice in traditional painting

Peace in Africa

Let there be peace in Africa.
Many African civilizations are suffering
from hunger and victims of the war.
Let there be peace in Africa.

Peace is based on justice.
Peace depends on the establishment
of justice and the respect for
the rights of all men and women.
Peace is not simply absence of war,
but is the fruit of justice and love.

Let there be peace in Africa.
We have to transform the Mentality
and dismantle the structures that
generate oppression of people.
Let there be peace in Africa.
Our beloved continent.
Our ancestors' land.

Samuel Manguale Apach   *Refugee from the Sudan in Kakumo Refugee Camp, Kenya (reprinted from Tilting Cages: An Anthology of Refugee Writings, edited and published by Naomi Flutter and Carl Solomon, Sydney, Australia, 1995, p.109)*

INJUSTICE

I know
You will not reveal to me
the origin of injustice
                    God
because You would not like others
to conquer your secrets.

But how do we justify
                the human actions?
How do we understand
                treason?
How do we assimilate
            an arbitrary law?

Justice arrives
thousands of years late.

Do not keep silent
                    God.
You cannot be an accomplice
of the cataclysms
of the world and its souls.
You cannot abandon us.

You should not.

Having been born
with this atavistic load
                of genocides
I became an expert
                on tragedies
especially one
                that You allowed
for I don't know
                what mysteries
of Your superhuman laws.

But I ask You
with this questionnaire
                of mortals

in which astral travel
are You engaged
when people are massacred?

In which alley of the universe
are You stuck
when the marks of impotence
of an entire race
are scattered in the deserts
or the concentration camps?

Where are You
            Almighty
when we need You
to say yes to our ancestry
with the vertical power
                of the roots.

Today we come
                to knock at Your door
to introduce our dreams
                to Your projects
because those
        who were exterminated
have a message
        for humankind.
An announcement
        of dialogue and peace
that needs Your hand
so that the mistakes
        are acknowledged.

Dilute from their shoulders
the weight of pain.

Make them forget
        how those submen
        pushed the caravans of death
                through the desert
or installed extinction
        in the gas chambers.

Your robe is white.
          Lord.
Cover sufferers with it
so their tears deviate
          from their course
and misery forgets its seal.

Join those causes
that belong to You
as much as the sorrow
          of the universe
Perhaps
in some fissure of time
when essences
          salute each other
justice
          will restore
               its debts.

One of them
will be paid for Der Zor [1]

I am still there.
Der Zor.
Silence and mystery.

A complete desert.

I swallow the silence
and I become its echo.

The peaceful mask
          of the Euphrates
has buried
          the true face
          of history.
But I still hear
          from the waves
          of old tragedies
screams
          gathered
              under the marble
              of the sacred chapel.

1 - Der Zor is the desert in Syria where Armenians were massacred by Turks.

The voices crystallize
the message engraved
on the uprooted cross-stones.
"We do not rest in peace
We do not rest in peace."

Standing in that desert
          where the sand
              oppresses each breath
I can see the black stones
          nourished
by the agony of my people.

Maddening pain
          still roaming
trying to find
          the peace
trapped
by the frozen sun.

Dust and sand.
The outside desert
gets inside you
and scratches your heart
with sandpaper claws.

One by one
the thorny laments
          slash
the walls of memory
and you can feel
          the anger
of the unburied bones
and you can hear
          the pounding
          of dried blood
jolting the earth.

Heaven has exploded
with injustice
and a rain of ashes
is crowing the weakness
drawing heavy tears

and burning the furrows
                    opened
on the flanks of death.

Abandoned temples
rise in my soul
and the veins of prayers
                    open
with a lonely ritual.

Thousands of screams
thundering through time
are carved here.

The rage of the universe
crushing the light
is condensed here.

The desert is burning
                    my feet
standing
          on the ashes
                    of our fathers.
If I could only soothe
one single pain.
But how
with what strength
could I root out
an endless anguish.

Dense furies
          are hardening
                    in my throat.
I want to shout.
Stand up!
Stand up within my soul
so I can cover
the burning ice
                    of the world
with my warm breath.

Come inside the altar
built by our people

to cure our orphaned roots
and destroy

the files of torture
sealed
          with poisoned wax.

Be in our dreams again
where you have always been
                    lifting the cross
                    impaled in our hearts.

Plow through the dessert
                    and stand up
so that today
at this very moment
we can go together
to pick up
all the scattered voices
                    of the earth
and compose
          the loudest song
to deafen the explosions.

And holding hands
          – with old blood
          and different skin –
climb the rays
          of all the suns
and create an Apocalypse

until a clear time
meets us in heaven.

Then we can weave
a future smile
and bell tolls
                    can announce
a new hallelujah!

... That our fathers
have been resurrected.
... that our people
                    are renewing
the dusty volumes
                    of history
and baptizing again
our own existence
as a message of new life.

On with our dreams!
On with our struggles!
Up to our victory!

But You know that now
the mothers of Artsakh [2]
are crying again
                    God
and children roam confused
searching for their fathers
                    among the dead
pleading for the war to end.

Yet their wishes are wounded
                    by the answers.

"Niet."
Absolutely no.
The order came from above.
Just the cold wind and snow
                    remained
in the corners of pain
to freeze the tears.

We must have lost our minds.

How can we call
what belongs to us
truly ours?
How can we bring it home?
Only
          lack and deprivation
          suffering and hurt
          slavery
          broken spines
can be ours.
We can only give
only bleed.

What else do we want?

Nothing
No thing

No.
It is a festival
                    of denial
                    and nothingness

The more I lengthen my voice
the further the listeners get.
The more I lengthen my hand
the further the future becomes.

                    My protest
                    is written as a poem
                    on the clouds.

But the protests stored
in my waiting people
are still marching
the avenues of rejection
and still picking up grief
along the way.

The kiss of life
          has dematerialized
and the Angel of Death
          is not pale any more
as in the vision of Turian [3]
it is colorful and bright
          nourished
with the red of Sumgait.[4]

And I feel my blood shaking
          struggling
not only inside my veins
          but bursting out
          running for miles
          to reach Karabagh
          and to join
the other half of my blood.

I am both.
          This one and that.
          Life and extinction.
The whole race lives inside me.
I bear in my enlarged heart
the children satiated
          with fear.

2 - Artsakh (or Karabach) is the historical Armenian territory for decades under the control of the Republic of Azerbaijan, which after much struggle and losses declared its independence.

3 - Bedros Turian is a well known Armenian poet. The themes of his poetry, while personal, apply to history and suffering of the people. He died in his early 20s of tuberculosis.

4 - Sumgait is the place where the Azeris massacred Armenians in 1989 at the start of the Nagorno-Karabagh conflict. The entire village of Simgait was massacred.

The people kneeling down
        on the ruins.

I am both.
        Here and there.
        Light and darkness.
The monster of gloom
        has shattered the houses
the souls inside the houses
the faith inside the souls.

At an insignificant
        corner of the map
a black vacuum
laden with cemeteries
                is reigning.

We push away the vacuum
but the cemeteries stay
as a satire of hope.

Everything is mixed up.
Today has become yesterday
yesterday... tomorrow.
We have been intoxicated
by the games of history
by the realism of illusion
when injustice is knocking
                at our doors
to drown our destiny.

How is it possible not to become
the abyss of existence
and not to feel absent
                from rights?
How can I restrain myself
from insulting justice?

For long years
our dried-out
dusty dreams
        were spread
        over forgotten graves
and the voice of stagnant time
        leaked silence

thick
deep
like a thought unwritten
        a pain untold.

That silence had made us deaf
and the impotence to speak
had choked our souls
with savage fingers.

But today
drained of eternal waiting
that same silence
        same impotence
has come out
from the cemetery crosses.
They have committed suicide
and have brought to life
        a fresh voice
with the alchemic truth
        of old voices
adding light
        to the new word
and injecting strength
        into the screams.

The throne of antisilence
        has been registered
                with courage.

Yes.
We need to talk.
Yes.
Our wounds are crying out
so the last particle on earth
can understand
        that there is no rest
                without justice.

Today
we have a date
        with human rights
        and we aspire
to look straight into the sun
even if in searching for light
        we get burned

even if we cannot
    measure the sky
      all at once.

Today
the imprisoned storms
    are freed
and the Voice of the Race
    breaks out
in spite of enemies.

God,
Let our screams
    be dispersed
      all over the world.
Let the truth of my people
echo through the waves
    of the universe
and let the rays
    of a different sun
declare without fear:

"Let people
    live in freedom!"

Then we will listen
to the just voices.

Thunder! Lighting!
The codes have exploded!

They say that claims
    will be heard
and a different law
    will renew
the rusted justice.

Do not execute
    the old verdicts.
Now the judges
    will be judged.

Heaven has discovered
    the truth
    piled up

    behind the clouds
to own the always.

They say the leader
comes in Your name
to recognize the rights.

They say new bibles
will throw to the fire
the old empty words
and its preachers
will no longer be
businessmen of the soul.

They say that finally
all the promises
will rise from their graves
    and shatter
the waiting hours.

And an essential peace
will unfold the questions
to conquer men.

There will be
    God
to testify for Your leadership,

Thunder! Lightning!
Do not execute the verdicts.

Heaven has finally opened
    its doors.

ALICIA GHIRAGOSSIAN
Born in Argentina to
Armenian parents
survivors of the 1915
genocide. Lawyer and poet,
Dr Ghiragossian's poetry
has earned international
prizes (reprinted from
Complete Works of Alicia
Ghiragossian. Interview
with God II, Ultimate
Mind Publishers,
California, USA, 1996)

"I will be in the forefront... to tell the world that I have the right to a homeland like the rest of the world's children."

SALWA IBRAHIM SAWALHA
15 years old, Palestinian native of Yebra, in Rafa refugee camp. This is one of a series of 19 paintings she did on the subject of the Intifada.

SUEÑO

Sueño
que estamos sentados
en la montaña solidaria
acobijados por el Sol
silbando nuestra armonía

Sueño
que nuestra ceguera
se convierte en un
relámpago del amanecer
y vamos despertando
para crecer

Sueño
que junto sembramos
y nuestra sementera
es frondosa como el ayer

Sueño
que escribimos
la paz en los surcos
del amor

Sueño
que admiro la
belleza de la alpaca
y jugamos con el agua
del manantial

Sueño
que estamos conversando
y reconstruyendo la vida
sin derramar más lágrimas
de temor y terror

Despierto
y vivimos envueltos
en una pesadilla
sin parar,
sin agua
se marchita nuestra
vida y libertad...

I AM DREAMING

I am dreaming
that we are sitting
on the mountain,
together in solidarity,
watched over by the sun,
whistling together in harmony.

I am dreaming
that our blindness
is becoming a lightning flash at
dawn,
and we are awakening
so as to grow.

I am dreaming
that together we shall sow seeds
and that the land we sow
is bearing lush crops
as it did in past days.

I am dreaming
that we are writing peace
in the furrows of love.

I am dreaming
that I am admiring
the beauty of the alpaca,
and that we are playing
in the waters of a spring.

I am dreaming
that we are talking with one another
and building life again
without shedding any more tears
of fear or terror.

I wake up...
and we are living surrounded
by an endless, arid nightmare,
and our life and freedom
are withering away...

*El autor es miembro de la
Comunidad Cristiana de
Desplazados, en el Perú Taller*

*The author is a member of the
Christian Community of Displaced
Persons, at the Peruvian Art
Workshop, 1996*

*(translated by the WCC Language
Service)*

CRY FOR PEACE

Chorus
Oh yes, my sisters and mothers don't be worried - x 2
You are subjected to this world of war
Yet you must focus on the future - x 2
There is hope-hope – deep in our hearts
that one day things will be alright - x 2
Hmm – Hmm – Hmm - - -

1st Solo
I know of a woman, who lived in a war zone
displaced from her happy home, to live in
a camp of poverty
She strived – strived all her life
Seeking only for the basic needs
She can only think of one essential fact
and that is to keep up her life.

2nd Solo
I know of a woman, who lost her occupation in war
She remained a non-working professional
Stirring up all ways to earn money
She tried – tried all this and that
Yet no luck or fortune came her way
She can only think of one essential fact
and that is to keep up her life.

3rd Solo
I know of a woman, who lost her husband in war
She remained a widow and a mother
of unlucky sons and daughters
She worked – worked all her life
to keep up her poor family
She can only think of one essential fact
and that is to keep her family's life.

Commentary

1. Life is all she is looking for
When is she expected to do any developmental
work for her community - x 2

No no – no! I know – I know
she has got no choice - x 4

2. War is the highest enemy
to any development
People lose all that they have built up
to the mercy of bombs and camps - x 2

Wooh – ya! We cry – we cry
again we cry – we cry for peace - x 4

Lamentations

1. O my people, o my God,
I was once a happy woman,
happily married, with a nice kid,
I lived a secured life in a good house.
But now – but now because of a merciless war,
I am forced to live a desperate life,
where the sky is my only shelter.
I tried to build this rumpled camp,
out of bits and pieces,
as the only security around my unprotected world.
But again here you come without sympathy
to destroy the little that I have.
Tell me my God, why all this suffering
why all this suffering – why – why – why!

2. O my God, why have you abandoned me,
listen to my cry o God.
Once I was the headmistress of a big school,
with a nice office and many school children around me.
At that time, I used to wear nice clothes with shoes on.
But now look at me, look at my clothes, look at my feet.
Where has everything gone – where are they –
where are they.

3. O my people, o my God,
I have lost my husband,
what can I give to my poor children,
I have nothing.
I am oppressed — I have no voice,
even if I speak no one hears me.
And now, my children have no school,
they cannot read or write,
they don't have a good shelter to sleep under,
nothing to eat, nothing to drink.
O my God, rescue me from this miserable life,
because you are my only helper.
O God, o God I need peace,
I need peace – peace – peace.

Summary Lamentations

Oh, I'm a widow, I've lost my husband.
I have no job. Yet I have children to look after.
I can't give them any shelter
nor can I give them food to eat.
Oh my poor children,
I can't stand about,
watching you die in bits from hunger and diseases,
Oh God, I pray that you bring peace.
I pray that you bring peace.
So that I can go back to the land of my ancestors,
Yes, back to the land of my ancestors

VICTORIA JABE ELUZAI

Sudanese from Southern Sudan, aged 25. The song was composed in Khartoum, Sudan, where she is living now as a displaced person from the South of Sudan. "I composed the lyrics since 1992. That was a time when I practically experienced the difficulty of being a displaced daughter and practically witnessed the tragic scene of displaced people being moved from one camp area to another. Then I lived with my widowed mother in one of the displaced people's camps. Outside the main city." "Cry for Peace" was first presented to the Sudan Council of Churches Women's Programme, First Christian Women Conference in June 1994.

DEM JUNGEN IM PARK   ## TO A BOY IN THE PARK

Junge
Lass die flügellose Taube
im Frieden
Schau mal
Ein Verbrecher machte
vom schönen Vogel
Einen Invaliden

Little boy
leave the wingless dove
in peace
Don't you see
some criminal has made the
lovely bird
a cripple

PALIC DERVIS
*Bosnischer Kriegsflüchtling, 29
Jahre alt, mit dem Status einer
Duldung, Deutschland*

Gib ihm ein Körnchen, zwei
Seine Freude soll auch
Deine werden

Give her a grain, or two
let her joy be yours
to share

PALIC DERVIS
*29-year old Bosnian refugee with
temporary status in Germany*

Junge
Berühre diese Taube nicht
solange sie träumt
Von der Höhe
Und dem Schwarm

Little boy
do not touch this dove,
let her dream
of the heights
and of the flight.

Helene Moussa

THE BROKEN PEACE

MOHAMMED MENSHAWI
*Baqu'a Palestinian Refugee Camp,
Jordan*

ARRÊTONS LA GUERRE

Je tends l'oreille à l'Est de mon pays
J'entends des cris
Des coups de canon par-ci
Des pleurs par-là
Des gens se meurent

Pour une histoire de goût et de couleur
Des vies entières s'écroulent
pour un échange de mots entre deux hommes
Des gens se meurent

A cet endroit jadis vivaient des hommes
qui partageaient la joie
Quand le démon de la guerre, un jour souffla
la flamme de la terreur

Au ciel la lune hésite
le soleil boude et les étoiles s'éteignent
sur ces enfants qui pleurent à leur côté
Des mères qui ne vivront plus.

REFRAIN *Arrêtons la guerre faisons la paix*
Rassemblons nos cœurs longtemps meurtris
Bientôt tout ce qui vit ne sera plus
Arrêtons la bagarre, finie la guerre
Arrêtons la loi du talion, faisons la paix

Arrêtons le sang des innocents
Il y a mieux à faire que faire des morts
Bientôt c'est la fin apocalypse
Arrêtons la vengeance, finit la haine
Arrêtons la loi du plus fort faisons la paix

La terre de ma nation est arrosée
Par le sang de mes frères
Victimes d'avoir aimé et partagé
le pain de l'amitié

La main que tu soulèves pour faire du mal
ne prendra plus ta défense

Let Us End the War

When I listen to the East of my country
I hear the sound of shouting
gunfire,
weeping,
people dying.

For a question of taste and colour
lives are being torn apart
for an exchange of words between two men
people are dying.

Once people lived together in this place
sharing their joys
until the day when the demon of war
unleashed the flame of terror

The moon in the sky is pale
the sun hides its face and the stars have gone out
over children weeping alone
beside their mothers who have died.

Refrain

Let's end the war, let's make peace
Let us unite to halt the long heartbreak
soon all living things will be silenced
Let's stop the fighting, put an end to war
Let's stop the law of eye for eye, and tooth for tooth and make peace

Let us stop the loss of innocent blood
There are better things to do than killing
soon will be the end of all things, apocalypse
enough of revenge, an end to the hatred
Let's have done with the law of the strongest and make peace

The soil of my land is soaked
with the blood of my brothers
who died because they loved and shared
the bread of friendship

The hand you raise to strike
can never defend you;

Car ce qu'on revendique par son épée
on le perd par son sang

Des petits enfants s'en vont sans revenir
perdus et étouffés dans la foule
loin de leurs parents qui ne pourront plus
jamais les retrouver
Au ciel la lune hésite, le soleil boude
Et les étoiles s'éteignent
sur ces enfants qui pleurent à leur côté
Des mères qui ne vivront plus.

Refrain

PAROLES
Karmela avait 13 ans lorsque la guerre frappa son village.
Une bombe explosa dans sa classe. Tous étaient morts; sauf lui.
Affolé par ce drame, il courait de toutes ses forces vers la maison
en criant «Maman! Maman!». Il heurta quelque chose dans le
couloir qui le fit tomber. C'était sa mère ! Couchée sur le dos, une
épée plantée dans son ventre. Pourtant, elle attendait famille. Il
fonça dans la chambre en appelant «Papa! Papa!». Et de la fenêtre,
il vit son père. Ou plutôt, le cadavre de son père. Et sur le manteau
qu'il portait on pouvait lire : Pendu pour avoir pleuré sa femme.

Une lumière s'éteint
L'horizon s'obscurcit. Le drame et l'opprobre de la Guerre.

LE CONTEUR   Viens Karmela ! Je connais un homme qui t'aime.
KARMELA   *Non! Personne ne m'aime. Et je n'aime personne.*
LE CONTEUR   Si, Karmela! Jésus t'aime
KARMELA   *Non! Il a vu ce qui s'est passé à l'école. Il était là quand ma mère est*
             tombée. J'ai perdu un frère qui allait naître et que j'avais appris à
             aimer. Il a laissé mourir mon père. Il m'a pris tout ce que j'avais.

             (Pleurs)

REFRAIN   *Oui Seigneur Jésus étends ta main*
             Et par ton Esprit viens consoler
             Tous ces cœurs meurtris et attristés
             Répands ta gloire Seigneur sur le Zaïre
             Et que ta volonté soit accomplie
             Répands ta gloire Seigneur sur l'Univers
             Et que ta volonté soit accomplie.

TEXTE ET MUSIQUE PAR
ALAIN MOLOTO
Kinshasha, novembre 1996

TEXT AND MUSIC BY
ALAIN MOLOTO
Kinshasa, November 1996

(translated by the WCC Language
Service)

what is won by the sword
is paid for in blood

Small children vanish, lost for ever,
crushed as the crowd
carries them away from parents
who will never see them again.

The moon in the sky is pale, the sun hides its face
and the stars have gone out
over children weeping alone
beside their mothers who have died.

REFRAIN   ...

VOICE   Karmela was 13 when the war struck his village. A bomb exploded
                 in his classroom. Everyone died – except him. Terrified by the
                 tragedy, he ran home as fast as he could, calling, "Mummy!
                 Mummy!" He stumbled over something in the corridor and fell. It
                 was his mother – lying on her back with a knife in her womb. Yet
                 she had been expecting a baby. He rushed into the bedroom
                 calling "Daddy! Daddy!" And from the window he saw his father.
                 Or rather, his father's body. And pinned to the coat he was
                 wearing the words, "Executed for mourning his wife."

                 A light goes out
                 The horizon grows dark. The tragedy and infamy of War.

NARRATOR   Come, Karmela ! I know a man who loves you.
KARMELA   *No you don't! No-one loves me. And I love no-one.*
NARRATOR   Yes, Karmela. Jesus loves you
KARMELA   *No he doesn't. He saw what happened at the school. He was there*
                 when my mother was killed. I've lost a brother who was about to be
                 born and I loved him. He let my father die. He's taken all I had.

                 (Weeping)

REFRAIN   *Stretch out your hand, Lord Jesus*
                 and by your Spirit come to comfort
                 all these sad and broken hearts
                 Lord, pour out your glory over our land Zaire
                 and may your will be done
                 Lord, pour out your glory over all the universe
                 and may your will be done.

ANMERKUNGEN ÜBER DEN MENSCHEN

NOTE ON HUMAN BEINGS

Wenn ich in den Himmel schaue
Hoch über mir
Wie klein bin ich im All

Schaue ich tief
in mich hinein
Wie das All klein ist in mir

When I look to the heavens
soaring above me
How small I am in the universe

When I look deep
within myself
How small is the universe in me.

St Andrew's Church African Arts and Crafts Programme, Cairo, Egypt

PALIC DERVIS
Bosnischer Kriegsflüchtling, 29 Jahre alt, mit dem Status einer Duldung, Deutschland

PALIC DERVIS
29-year old Bosnian refugee with temporary status in Germany

(translated by the WCC Language Service)

SUDANESE COUNTRYSIDE

LAKEW SAMUEL LAKEW
Painter and poet, born in 1971, refugee from Southern Sudan in Egypt. He unexpectedly died of a heart attack in January 1998. He had no formal training in fine arts. He was painting in the African Arts and Craft programme. His paintings chiefly depicted images of peace and tranquillity that he dreamed could be restored to his homeland.

WOULD THERE BE AN END TO OUR PATHETIC SITUATION ?

The story of Eelam is unending
whilst there is never a liberation for us.
For ever there is a rain of fire
and unnumbered Trials and Tribulations.
Tender shoots of our younger generation
have been sacrificed on the altar of conflict
Unable to reach portals of Education
and taste the fruits of knowledge
our youths have fallen prey
to cruel and inhuman tormentors' schemes.
Bharat too has taken no notice,
neither has the minds of villains softened.
God too appears to have turned a blind eye,
our eyes too have no tears left for crying.
When oh when! venerable sage
the pathos of our situation will come to an end?

TAMIL V. NAGASAKTHY

A refugee from Sri Lanka, she is a coaching class teacher in the Irumpoothipatty refugee camp, Tamil Nadu, India. She is also following a bachelor of commerce degree under the correspondence course scheme of the university. She has one elder brother and one younger brother and two younger sisters. The family ekes out an existence through the dole given by the Indian government and the small income from the sale of lottery tickets by the father.

How shall We sing the Lord's Song in a Strange Land ?

Many times when I listen to the radio and read the newspapers, I hear bishops, preacher men and other holy men of God calling on Liberians to live a life of honesty, a life of love, peace and unity.

But how can we sing the Lord's song in a strange land? How can we sing the Lord's song in a land where people prefer Barnabas, the crook, to Jesus the man of truth and justice; a land where the rich who steal and donate money to good causes are praised, and the poor are despised?

The song of truth is the Lord's song. We cannot sing it in this strange land. The melody of honesty is the Lord's song. We cannot sing it in this strange land.

The tune of forgiveness is the Lord's tune. We cannot hum it in a strange land. A land where those who have killed demand to be praised and rewarded with leadership of the country.
The Lord's song is a song of love, peace, unity and harmony. It is not possible to sing it in a land that has become so polarized by injustice and human right abuses that war seems acceptable.

If you like to hear us sing the Lord's song, take us home to the holy land, where the prophets say what God tells them, not what the king or the mob would like to hear. The land where pastors live what they preach, not where they tell you by their behaviour "do what I say but don't do what I do".

Take us to the land flowing with milk and honey.

This is the song of the captives by the rivers of blood in the "sweet of Liberty".

A Liberian refugee working with Jesuit refugee Service Liberian Working Group
(reprinted from Jesuit Refugee Service, An Occasional Newsletter, no. 15, 1996, p.14)

Photogravure: clairoset

Un Monde à Reconquérir

Sur ce fond de cordillière, que l'on a retrouvé si souvent dans les Arpilleras, un couple s'avance vers l'avenir. Malgré l'oppression représentée ici par les camps de prisonnier et les maisons de torture, les parents veulent, pour eux et leurs enfants, retrouver un chemin de paix et d'amour.

Against the backgound of the Cordillera, which we find again and again in the cloths, a couple is walking towards the future. In spite of the oppression, depicted here by prison camps and houses of torture, the parents are trying to find the way back to a life of peace and love for themselves and for their children.

(reprinted from André Jacques, Chili un peuple brode sa vie et ses luttes, CIMADE, Paris, 1977)

Send My Soul Abroad

Oath, hypocritic oath,
One thing for me to loath,
You in a mere mask, sheer veneer
'Tis wake up call, don't ever err
Unleash this sordid error
Don't just hate it, but abhor.

Live your ancestors call
When Adam and Eve were able
Before their eyes were open
While they were aboriginal
Created in God's image
And knew not they were abject
And ever since they lived short of their master's words;
Hypocrisy entered the world, and oath replaced truth.

Lord, as you regretted your own works
I also hate the pattern, I also curse
Make me not be, nor do I see
One pretending, do hypocrisy.
Send my soul abroad
Where I live naked
And finish the unaccomplished

An Ethiopian, born on 6 April 1972, who worked as a journalist on the only English-language newspaper in Addis Ababa until his opposition to the regime caused him to lose his job. He subsequently fled and sought asylum in Italy. He wrote this poem in English on 20 April 1996 in Italy.

Zecharias Getahun Mogessie

Let's Go in Peace

Thousands stretched out their hands,
risked their lives and sought refuge
only to be trapped by immigration laws.
Years ate up hopes and dreams,
unanswered questions gnawed their souls.
But so called diplomats sail smoothly within days
what the common man struggles through years –
yet unsolved and unsettled.
Clogged, logged and put on hold,
their life set at pause or freeze.
Running from nightmares and waking to hearings,
their humaneness denied and destroyed,
beings see another year slip by – unlived.
Logged lives come alive to shed tears
for another who has decided to die.
Years of inaction sparks into action
decision to die than indefinitely hang.

How much more grief can we bear?
How much more proof need we bare?
What will make you believe or decide,
Our mangled bodies or our tortured souls?
As a last resort I beg you and you,
Am I not eligible for even a chance to live?
disconnect the immigration backlog – NOW.

Sudharshana Coomarasamy

May 1991

In memory of Jesus Seferino Aguilar, a refugee claimant who committed suicide, and remembering many others whose lives are on hold. Sudharshana Coomarasamy fled Sri Lanka in 1984 with her 8-month old twins and was a church-sponsored refugee in Canada 1986. She is an active advocate of the rights of refugee and immigrant women.

CHAPTER FIVE
STRUGGLING TOGETHER FOR HOPE

The Dream in Focus

If I have the power to perform
I will surely have a will to reform.
To see my dreams in uniform
truly Banaba will take a new form.

Some like to give and some like to take
And for my elders who gave it was a mistake.
Surely my dreams recoil as a snake
Oh Banaba why did they have to forsake.

All our land has been taken and stolen
The beauty once green is now broken
But my dream only grows to let the whole world know,
Of Banaba our homeland, our spirit is never broken.

KEN SIGRAH BANABAN
1998

Born on the new island of Rabi in 1956. He is a clan spokesperson and historian for Banaban clan elders on Rabi. He is currently in Australia working on a Banaban history – the first book to be written by a Banaban – The People of Banaba.

Ocean Island is approximately two and a half square miles situated near the Equator in the central Pacific and inhabited by an indigenous race known as the Banabans. In 1900 rich deposits of phosphate were discovered, and the British Phosphate Commission (made up of the United Kingdom, Australian and New Zealand governments) exploited these resources until 1980. During the second world war the island was invaded and occupied by Japanese forces; Banabans were murdered and the survivors deported to other Pacific islands under Japanese control. When the war was over the Banabans were gathered on Tarawa Island and told they could not return to their homeland because their food crops and houses had been destroyed. The British Phosphate Commission restarted phosphate mining and used this as the excuse to move the Banabans to Fiji. The British government had purchased Rabi Island from Lever Brothers just prior to the outbreak of the war, using the Banabans' own provident fund money, as they knew eventually they would need to mine all of Banaba. On 15 December 1945, 703 Banabans and 300 Gilbertese arrived on Rabi Island in Fiji, where they were left in army tents with two months of food rations. The rest is history.

Asylum Seekers Centre

ATTIC WINDOW[1]

This piece of artwork with universal modern contemporary characteristics was designed and painted by ten asylum-seekers in Brisbane, Australia. They came from China, Columbia, Iran, Liberia, Lebanon, Turkey, Romania and the former USSR. Painted with expressions and colours peculiar to their country of origin, it reflects past and current experiences. Domingo Montenegro, a professional artist from Mexico and former refugee, tutored the asylum-seekers as they worked on this mural. His works of art are known internationally, and the Queensland Art Association selected his work for the launch of their new policy in 1995. The mural was launched at Refugee Week, 1996; it was dedicated to all Australians and social organizations that help to make real a new life for those in the world who need support and love.

1 - An attic is where you put the old things you don't need any more. Old things bring memories... this mural brought back memories... Moved old things in my heart. But now we are co-existing here... learning together, living together. The window is our interpretation, our perception. With our thinking, feeling eyes we look to the future.

ATTIC WINDOW

I am happy with the teachers
with friendship, peace and new hopes.

I want to understand English to make
many friends in the future
This is my dream !

I want to live in my country
But I can't !
I would like to live in Australia and on the earth.
Can I ?

But my house has been set on fire
and I can't return in there.
I know there is freedom
But not in my country !

Destruction, foreign powers, huge
pressure, it is not my people's ambition.

The desire to express our decisions in our country
led to the absence of bread... many executions.

Our freedom, person's opinions and human
rights does exist in my country ?

Severe punishment leading to death
It is the true democracy ?

I am a human, I don't want to see the agony of the
hungry, the tragedies and destruction in my life
all that I want, is to live in peace
and enjoy my life.

GEORGE
An asylum-seeker in Australia

Untitled

Rihab Abbas, 1996
*Refugee between the ages of 9-15 living in a Gaza refugee camp and attending elementary
school for girls. One of the prize-winning drawings on the theme of "Keep Gaza beautiful
and clean."*

Niños de la CPR

En las escuelas de esta montaña
nuestros niños aprenden la verdad
organizados y siempre contentos
son el futuro de la nueva sociedad.

En el principio no había recurso
fue un poco duro empezar a enseñar
pero ahora algo se ha mejorado
con la mano de la solidaridad.

Nuestros niños en la resistencia
aprenden también la igualdad
entre ellos no hay diferencia
y respetar a todos por igual.

En el alma yo llevo a estos niños
a quienes quiero y no puedo olvidar
estaré para siempre con ellos
resistiendo en la selva del Ixcán.

*Comunidades de Población en Resistencia
"Comunidad Primavera del Ixcán" Finca San
Isidro, Ixcán Quiché, Guatemala, CA*

Children of the PRC*

In the schools in these mountains
our children are learning the truth.
Organized, always content,
they are the future of our new society.

At first, there were no resources.
It was quite difficult to start teaching.
But now things are better
with solidarity's helping hand.

Our children in the resistance movement
are also learning equality.
There are no differences between them,
and they respect everyone as equal.

I carry these children in my heart.
I love them, cannot forget them
I shall be with them for ever
resisting in the forest of Ixcán.

**People's Resistance Communities, Springtime
Community of Ixcán, San Isidro Estate, Ixcán Quiché,
Guatemala, Central America*

(translated by the WCC Language Service)

TOUS UNIS NOUS ABATTRONS CE RAPACE DE MALHEUR

United we will defeat this greedy vulture of misfortune

reprinted from André Jacques, Chili, un peuple brode sa vie et ses luttes, CIMADE, Paris,
1977

LAS MUJERES EN LA RESISTENCIA

Todas sabemos que en Guatemala
se sufre tanto por la explotación,
las violaciones de los derechos,
dura y amarga discriminación.

Como mujeres en resistencia
en busca de nuestra liberación,
nos reunimos un día veinte,
mes de septiembre del noventa y uno.

En asambleas, muy decididas,
todas hablamos de la situación
En ese día, la OMR
nació dispuesta para luchar.

Por nuestra vida, nuestra cultura,
por nuestros hijos, nuestra nación
hoy avanzamos en nuestra lucha
valientemente en CPR.

En las tareas comunitarias
participamos ahora mejor
hoy caminamos con gran confianza
con las ideas de los abuelos.

Que nos dejaron sabiduría,
hermoso ejemplo de resistencia
Llegue la aurora y que amanezca
¡Oh Gran abuela, Ixmucané!

*Comunidades de Población en Resistencia
"Comunidad Primavera del Ixcán" Finca San
Isidro, Ixcán Quiché, Guatemala, C.A.*

(translated by the WCC Language Service)

WOMEN IN THE RESISTANCE MOVEMENT

We all know that in Guatemala
there is much suffering,
because of exploitation,
human rights violations
and cruel, harsh discrimination.

Seeking our liberation,
as women in resistance
we met together on the twentieth
of September ninety-one.

We were very determined and
in our meeting
we all discussed the situation.
On that day the WRO[1]
was born, prepared to struggle,

For our life, for our culture,
for our children, for our nation.
Today we go bravely forward in our struggle
in the People's Resistance Communities.

We are now better at sharing together
in our communal tasks.
We are travelling on
with immense confidence,
following the ideas of our ancestors.

They left us a legacy of wisdom,
a beautiful example of resistance.
Let daybreak come! Let a new day dawn!
Oh great ancestor, Ixmucané!

*People's Resistance Communities, Springtime Community
of Ixcán, San Isidro Estate, lxcán Quiché, Guatemala,
Central America*

1 - Women's Resistance Organization

St. Andrew's Church African Arts and Crafts Programme, Cairo, Egypt

HARMONY AND LOVE

TAMERAT ABEBE
"This painting expresses two feelings. It is a song with its rhythmical lines to make you listen and love at the same time." Tamerat Abebe is an Ethiopian refugee in Egypt. Born in 1968 he graduated from the Fine Arts School in Addis Ababa, Ethiopia, in 1993. In Egypt he gives art classes to other African refugees. His works have been exhibited in Egypt where he has received several certificates of recognition at national and international events.

Untitled

1994

Goran Chirco

13-year old Iraqi Kurd refugee in Lebanon. He did this drawing in a class taught by Iraqi adult artists who were also refugees in that country. The class was part of a programme of the Middle East Council of Churches Service to Refugees, Displaced and Migrants (SRDM)

In der Liebe

In der Liebe
Vom Lachen bis zu den Tränen
Fehlt kaum ein Augenblick

In der Liebe
Vom Gesang bis zum Schweigen
Fehlt kaum ein Aufeinanderklatschen
der Hände

In der Liebe
Von der Liebe bis zum Hass
Fehlt kaum ein Schritt.

Der Gläubige

In mir
Die Leere von Irrwegen
Dein Wort
Lebte auf

Jetzt kenne ich das Geheimnis
Des Schmetterlings
Welcher zum Lichte eilt

PALIC DERVIS
Bosnischer Kriegsflüchtling, ist 29 Jahre alt mit
dem Status einer Duldung, Deutschland

In Love

In love
from laughter to tears
is but a moment

In love
from song to silence
is but a handclap

In love
from love to hate
is but a step

The Believer

In me
the emptiness of erring ways
Your Word
came alive

Now I know the secret
of the moth
that strains towards the light.

PALIC DERVIS
29-year old Bosnian refugee with temporary status
in Germany

(translated by the WCC Language Service)

MOTHER EARTH

Oh mother who radiates beauty
When can I repose on thy bosom?
My grieving heart cannot be comforted
To see you scattered and destroyed.
Where is the Garden that bloomed fair blossoms.
And the fields that brought forth grain aplenty?

When day light gets covered in darkness,
The clouds bring forth showers of rain.
However, what is the wonder of thy struggle
For the sunrise of hope to banish dark forebodings?
The enmity which causes darkness to descend
Can be driven away by the milk of human kindness.

Words that bring comfort, solace and peace
should be understood to wipe away sorrow and sadness.
The trials and tribulations of the people of Eelam
Who will throw light to drive away the darkness?

Thousands of innocent Tamil people in Eelam
are being pathetically maimed and killed.
Mother to thy bosom I rush like a waterfall,
So that you may gather all the Tamil people together
To stop the gushing blood from the wounds inflicted.

C.L. KANAKARATNAM
Ilrumboothipatti refugee camp,
Tamil Nadu, India. A Tamil
refugee from Sri Lanka, C.L.
Kanakaratnam is a teacher in the
refugee camp. Her husband and
three children are with her
(translated from Tamil by
Organization for Eelam Refugee
Rehabilitation OfERR)

Today or tomorrow, we look with expectation,
for a just solution to befit our sacrifices,
The days are fast fleeing past us
O mother to thee we come to unburden our sorrows and wail.
Do cover us with wings of solace and comfort as only a mother can do.

When my final resting days approach,
My mortal remains shall become,
Dust to dust and ashes to ashes to enrich the fields,
For saplings to sprout in the morning of hope.

Ecumenical Women's Solidarity Fund, WCC, Zagreb, Croatia

DANCE IN WATERCOLOURS

HILDA DUGONJIC MIJATOVIC
*Born in Vares, Bosnia and
Herzegovena. During the war
years she fled to to Novo Mesto in
Slovania with a teenage daughter
and her husband, invalided
following serious injuries during the
war. In Vares she worked as a
teacher of art and culture in the
town's primary school and ran an
art gallery. In the refugee camp she
worked as a volunteer teacher for
two years, where she held creative
workshops. Many of her works have
been shown in solo exhibitions.*

CLAP AND DANCE FOR THE DAWN OF LIFE

Clap and dance my damsel
Dance to let the good times be born
Clap and dance again
Let the good times be born.

Let there be love, dance for that
Let there be growth of culture
dance for that too
Dance for all the good to come
and dance for the birth of Tamil Eelam.   *(clap and dance...)*

Let all the sorrows disappear
Dance for the birth of heaven
Let there be no anger and
Let all good qualities be invoked.   *(clap and dance...)*

Dance for the end of all destruction
Dance for the birth of freedom and peace
Let all sins and revenge be forgotten
and let the clean and clear path open out.   *(clap and dance...)*

Dance for the preservation of all our rights
Let good feelings fill the reservoir of peace
Dance so that the darkness is dispelled
and for the dawn of a great future.   *(clap and dance...)*

Words adapted to Indian refugee situation from a Tamil folk nursery song and set to music in Tamil by Eelathu Ratnam (translated from Tamil by V. Kallayapillai)

Eelathu Ratnam produced Tamil and Sinhala films. In 1983 he fled to Tamil Nadu, India, where he joined, as a volunteer, the Organization of Eelam Refugee Rehabilitation (OfERR). He died in a tragic accident in 1994. The refugees at the camp where he was have continued to use song and poetry to express themselves.

Bienvenue Automne

Warmth of the sun
warmed
then burnt
Tanned and grilled
we closed our eyes
Unaware autumn had crept behind us.
Now trees are shedding leaves –
golden,
like the dreams of youth
or
like people shedding
their suntanned skins,
we lose lustre and grow pale.
Grow pale at the thought of the future:
flurries, snowstorms, boots and shovels,
laws, legislations and rejections.
Yet within us echoes
the promise of spring and summer sun.
Always this little voice of hope
springs, warms, and blooms,
hurts, heals and grows.
This year and the next
again and again
without rest,
we bloom, fade and fall
only to bloom again –
ready for another fall.

Sudharshama Coomarasamy
Montreal, September 1987

Fled Sri Lanka in 1984 with her 8-months old twins and was a church-sponsored refugee in Canada in 1986. She is an active advocate of the rights of refugee and immigrant women. This poem was written on the occasion of the new Canadian immigration bills C55 and C84 restricting refugee entry into the country (reprinted from Intricate Countries: Women Poets from Earth to Sky, 1996, pp.53-54, published by Artemis Enterprises, RR#2, Box 54, Dundas, Ontario, Canada L9H 5E2, Artemis@icom.ca)

The following play was written, starred in and directed by the Japanese Filipino children of the Batis Centre for Women in the Philippines. After attending a theatre workshop facilitated by a local theatre group, the children's play was staged during the National Theater Youth Festival in Intramuros, Manila, 6-8 February 1998. These children are born of Filipino mothers working in Japan and Japanese fathers; they have most often been abandoned by their fathers.

VESTIGES OF THE PAST :
A JAPANESE FILIPINO CHILDREN STORY

Scriptwriter	Heidi Sato, 13
Translation	from the Filipino by Ava Gonzales, a Batis volunteer
Director	Junko Lorraine Yamamoto, 15
Production designers	Shigeo Hasumi, 15
	Ryuji Yamamoto, 14
	Takeyoshi Tomita, 13
Stage manager	Lorna San Buenaventura, a Batis social worker

LEAD CHARACTERS

Aiko Yamada, 14	as Jaja, a Japanese Filipino child born in the Philippines and fortunate enough to experience to love of both her parents. Although her Japanese father eventually separated from her Filipina mother, Jaja is registered in Japan and her father continues to provide financial support for her.
Maiko Hagita, 14	as Liza, a Japanese Filipino child born in Japan who has yet to meet her Japanese father. She has an abusive Filipino stepfather and a full-blooded Filipino brother and sister.

1 - A term used in the Philippines for Overseas Contract Worker

Junichi Kanezuka, 14   as Yoshi, a Japanese Filipino child born in Japan whose father refuses to acknowledge him.

CAST
Junko Yamamoto *as Yoshi's mother and Jaja's mother (dual roles)*
Ryuji Yamamoto *as Yoshi's father and Jaja's father (dual roles)*
Shirley Canaria, *16, as Liza's mother*
Mikas Aleya Matsuzuwa, *11, as Jaja's cousin*
Siegi Maeda, *10, as Liza's (full-blooded Filipino) half brother*
Arian Valencia, *10, as Liza's (full-blooded Filipino) half sister and the young Jaja (dual roles)*
Shin Imai, *11, as the young Yoshi Kenji Yamamoto, 12, as the policeman*
Tetsuya Yoshino, *9, as Jaja's cousin Heidi Sato as a Batis social worker.*

The students taking their Nighonggo (Japanese) lessons go to school. Takeyoshi, Iza and Shigeo are seated at centre stage, playing the flute while preparing for a tea ceremony.

Liza and Jaja enter. They have kimonos with them. They show the others how the kimono is worn, and after putting on the kimono Yoshi and Shin enter, with their kimonos already on. Arian and Mikas enter, also wearing kimonos, with a tray of tea. Liza and Jaja pour tea into the cups and Mikas and Arian give the tea to Yoshi and Shin who drink the tea together and say:

Shin and Yoshi   How delicious!

All the students shout and jump around saying: "Hurrah! We now know how a tea ceremony goes!"

Yoshi   Let's clean up this mess first.

Seigi   That's right, so we can get started already.

Jaja   Let's practise the song sensei (teacher) taught us.

Liza	Okay.
All the students	*fall in line in facing the audience, getting ready to sing the song.*
Liza	Okay, let's get ready now. Ready, one, two, three...
All the students	*sing the Japanese song together.* *Okina kurino kinoshitade* *Anata to watashi* *Nakayoku asobimasho* *Okina kurino kinoshitade* *There is a big tree* *You and me* *Let us play in the big tree* *In the big tree let us play*
Yoshi	Would you like us to teach them [the audience] the song?
Jaja	That would be nice!
Jaja	Let's read the lyrics first before we teach them how to sing it.
Shirley	Wait! We should explain what the song means before we sing it.
Junko	She's right.
All the students	*read the song out loud.*
Liza	We'll sing the song line by line first and you can sing each line after us.
Jaja	Now, let's sing the whole song.

Heidi	I think it would be better if we put some action in the song.
Arian	That's right. Let's all stand up *(referring to the audience)*
Shin	*(Whispers with all the other children)* Right! It is better if we put some action in the song.
Liza	Are you ready? One, two, three!
Everyone	sings along, with the matching action.
All the students	That was great!
Shirley	*(addressing the audience)* Did you like that?

The bell rings and...

Shirley	Wait a minute, there goes the bell. We'll have to sing the song later.
Arian	*(addressing the audience)* We should all be seated first. We are going to have our recess.

The students run around and play during recess, exiting one by one. Only Yoshi, Jaja and Liza are left on stage. Liza and Jaja see Yoshi looking sullen and all by himself in a corner.

Jaja	Hey, Yoshi, why don't you want to go out yet?
Liza	Yeah, Yoshi, why don't you want to have recess yet? Let's go!
Yoshi	Nothing. I just remembered something.

Liza	What's bothering you?
Yoshi	Promise you can keep a secret? This is just going to be between the three of us, okay?
Jaja	Don't you trust us? Aren't we friends?
Liza	Come over here and tell us the secret.

Yoshi begins to tell his story.

| Yoshi | You know me – you know that my mother worked in Japan and it was where she met my father. |

Yoshi's mother enters. She is in a train station. Yoshi's father enters afterwards...

| Yoshi | The minute my mother saw my father, she fell in love. |

Yoshi's mother and Yoshi's father hold hands.

| Yoshi | I remember very well that my father loved my mother very much. |

Yoshi's mother pirouettes on stage. Yoshi's dances along with her. Yoshi's mother kneels and offers her partner the baby she holds in her arms.

Yoshi	Until my mother gave birth to me.
Yoshi's father	We have a handsome son.
Yoshi's mother	Of course. He takes after us, you being handsome and me being beautiful.
Yoshi	We were as happy as we could be. But one day... my father disappeared.

Yoshi's father leaves. Yoshi's mother becomes frightened, panics on stage. She and her son have now become illegal immigrants in Japan.

Yoshi's mother   My son, what is to become of us? We are illegal aliens in this country. We have no home. Where are we to go? What is to become of us now?

The police knock at their door.

Police   This is immigration.

Yoshi's mother   (*Very distressed*) Oh no! They're here! They're going to make us leave.

Yoshi   We had to leave for the Philippines, and that was where I grew up.

The young Yoshi enters, playing with a basketball. Arian sees him and teases him...

Arian   Half-breed Japanese brat! Half-breed Japanese brat! Half-breed Japanese brat!

The young Yoshi   What's your problem? Do you want a punch from me?

Arian   Grandmother, grandmother, the Japanese boy is picking a fight with me!

Arian's grandmother comes out to defend her grandson and berates Yoshi.

Arian's grandmother   Young man, do you know what you're doing to my grandson? Why are you fighting him? It must be the Japanese blood in your veins. (*She leaves with her grandson*)

The young Yoshi is left behind. He sits with the basketball still in his hands.

Yoshi   Ever since I could remember it was always that way. I kept getting into fights while growing up.

Liza and Jaja try to comfort their friend.

Yoshi   Is being half-Japanese so bad? I have to be grateful I am a whole human being. What's wrong with me? I'm nice. I'm intelligent. Not to mention handsome. *(looking around)* Oh, they've gone.

Yoshi approaches Liza and Jaja.

Yoshi   Do you know that I was given the chance to see my father?

Jaja   How lucky you are!

Yoshi   What do you mean, lucky? I haven't finished telling you my story! One day...

The young Yoshi enters with his mother.

Yoshi's mother I'm bringing you to meet your father.

Young Yoshi   Do I look like him?

Yoshi's mother You have the same eyes.

Yoshi's father arrives with papers he hands over to Yoshi's mother.

Yoshi's father   I'm sorry I cannot sign this paper. I'm not even sure that this boy is really my son. I'm sorry.

Yoshi's father turns to leave.

Yoshi's mother holds her son close to her. Crestfallen, they turn their backs.

Yoshi	It was difficult. I love my father, but why can't he accept me as I am in return?
Jaja	Yoshi, your father is not the only one capable of giving you love. There are many people who love you. Your grandmother and mother love you very much. We, your classmates will always be here if you ever need anything.
Liza	She's right, Yoshi. We love you.
Yoshi	Really? You love me?
Jaja	Uyyy. Do I smell romance in the air?
Liza	*(spanks Yoshi)* Of course not. We all belong in one organization and it's just right for us to love each other. You're lucky, you at least got to see what your father looks like.
Yoshi	Haven't you seen your father yet?
Liza	No, I didn't even get the chance to meet him.
Jaja	Maybe you would like to share your story with us. We don't have a clue about your life.
Liza	*(tells her story)* Okay. But you promise not to tell anyone else?
Jaja	Okay.

Liza	I was born in Japan, but my mother and father did not live together. That is why we left for the Philippines. My mother got married again and I have two half-brothers from her marriage to a Filipino.

Arian and Seigi enter.

Liza	Have you done your homework yet?
Arian	Opo, ate. *(loosely translated as "yes, my dear sister"; "Opo" is a formal Filipino yes, used for someone of higher position, authority, or power as a sign of respect; "Ate" is used to address on older female sibling)*
Seigi	Ate, my friends are asking why you are mestiza *(light-skinned)* while Arian and I are negro *(black-skinned)*?
Liza	Don't mind them. Don't you know that black is beautiful?
Arian	Ate, if I need help with my homework. I'll call you over.

While Arian and Seigi are busy doing their homework, Liza's stepfather calls her.

Liza's stepfather	Liza, I told you to clean the bathroom. I don't want to see the bathroom dirty.
Liza	I'm sorry father, I haven't finished what I'm doing yet.
Liza's stepfather	Don't you dare call me father. Enough of your flimsy excuses. Go on, and clean the bathroom.

Liza	Opo, Itay. *(loosely translated as "Yes, father")*

Liza cries while cleaning the bathroom.

Liza's mother	Liza, where are your brother and sister? Are they doing their homework?
Liza	Opo, Inay. *(loosely translated as "yes, mother")*
Liza's mother	Why are you crying?
Liza	Father has never ceased scolding me.
Liza's mother	I told you so. That's what you get for being so stubborn. You never listen to him.

Liza's mother leaves, and Liza cries all by herself.

Liza	*(to herself)* They always scold me.
Liza's stepfather	Liza! What's going on? Clean the bathroom well. Wash the dirty plates afterwards. Give your brother and sister their baths. Clean the rooms. Don't forget to cook our meal...

To each request, LIZA answers "Opo, Itay". She is harassed by her stepfather's many orders.

Liza	*(screaming)* I can't take it anymore!
Liza's stepfather	What? Are you talking back? *(pushes Liza)* Remember your place. I feed you and let you stay here even if you aren't my own flesh and blood.
Liza's mother	I told you so. Liza, if you just listened to me, we could have prevented this. You

know very well that your stepfather has been so generous to let us eat and sleep here. It doesn't do him justice whenever you disobey his orders.

Liza   Mother, why is he always scolding me? I can't seem to do anything right.

Liza's mother   That's the trouble with you, Liza. You always talk back, even when you know that you're at fault. That's the kind of attitude that angers your stepfather even more.

Liza's mother leaves and...

Liza   I couldn't take it anymore so I ran away from home.

Yoshi   Where did you go?

Jaja   Do tell us where you went, Liza.

Heidi, the social worker from Batis, enters.

Heidi   Here at Batis we can help you. We can send you to school and we can bring you back to your family whenever they are ready to accept you back.

Liza   I still love my mother and father very much, but I'm not ready to go back to them yet.

Jaja   Quit moping around. A beautiful future is awaiting all of us.

Yoshi   Really?

Jaja   Even I had a chance to be happy. Even I know how it feels to be loved by one's parents. My mother and father stayed together for a little while here in the Philippines. We were very happy then. How was I to know that the moment my father left for Japan, it would be the last time I would see him and that I would grow up here in the Philippines?

The young Jaja enters.

Young Jaja	Grandmother, grandmother!
Jaja's grandmother	My grandson, have you seen the rice cakes and sweet potatoes that I prepared for you?
Young Jaja	Grandmother, grandmother, please tell me a story about the Magic Kingdom!
Jaja's grandmother	I know a better story. I'll tell you the story of Judy and Santos's soap opera, where she plays the role of a little girl named Esperanza.
Young Jaja	Alright, grandmother.
Jaja	I was also blessed enough to experience what it was like to be loved by a grandmother and cousins.

Jaja's cousins and friends enter.

Seigi	Mano po, lola. *(Loosely translated as "bless me, grandmother"; the Filipino practice of "mano" is a gesture of showing respect to an elder: a young person gently takes the hand of the elder person, bringing the fingers of the older person to his or her forehead; the "mano" is also known as the "kissing of the hand")*

Tetsuya	Mano po, lola. Let's go fishing in the river!
Seigi	Let's go swimming as well.
Young Jaja	Grandmother, we're going now.
Jaja's grandmother	Okay, hurry along, just make sure to come home before it gets dark.
All the children	Yes, grandmother.
Jaja	Like you, Yoshi, I also had the chance to see my father.
Jaja's mother	Jaja, I'm going to let you meet your father. But I hope you understand that your father and I can never live together again because he has a family in Japan to think about.
Young Jaja	Yes, mother.
Jaja's father	*(in Japanese)* Amelia, how are you?
Jaja's mother	*(responding in Japanese)* I am fine.
Jaja's father	Is this Jaja, my daughter?
Jaja's mother	Yes.

Young Jaja kisses the hand *("mano")* of her father.

Jaja's father	She is a good girl. Here are the papers I have signed. I am now willing to recognize, register and support Jaja.
Jaja's mother	Thank you very much.
Jaja's father	I hope you understand.

Jaja   See, all of us share similar stories. We all
                    don't have fathers. Even so, it's not an
                    excuse to mope around. You've moped
                    around so much that now you're beginning
                    to look like Andrew E. *(A popular Filipino
                    singer-comedian)*

Recess isn't over yet and all the children call Yoshi, Liza and Jaja
to join them.

Shirley   Haven't you had recess yet?

Jaja   Hey, wait a minute, we promised to show
                    them *(the audience)* something.

All the children dance a Japanese dance before waving and exiting
from the stage.

THE STEADFASTS
1989

Painting by Hamdan Mohammed El Banna, Jaffa. Born in 1956

JEDDAH
ON MY WAY HOME

In my heart engraved
    thousands of feelings
    Collected and spelt
    As I trod your roads and paths
    Among a few who dared.

In my brain engraved
    Countless thoughts
    reflected and formed
    As I mingled
    With your people's
    Wounds and dirt.

In my soul are treasured
    The millions of secrets
    Folded and cherished
    As I kissed and embraced
    The ecstasy of your sunrise
    And sunsets.

In my veins roar
    Sea of blood
    Gushing hopelessly
    As I view in your mirror
    The distorted face
    Of my homeland.

In my hands stones of wisdom
    Gripped and clenched
    As I retreat
    Deeper into your bosom
    To calculate momentum...
    To the unchaining back home.

MAE ROCA, JEDDAH 1987
*(reprinted from T.N.T. trends, news
and tidbits, official newsletter of
Kanlungan Centre Foundation
Centre for Migrant Workers,
Quezon City, Philippines)*

An OCW's[1] Wife's Prayer

River of tears have found their way,
With heavy heart one night I knelt to
pray;
"Heavenly Father, please hear my plea,
Protect my husband while he is away."
Provide us both with faithful hearts,
Firm and resistant to every evil's dart,
Making no room for loneliness
Or else our lives will be a mess.
Keep us busy with our life's cares,
From doubts and worries our minds
do spare,
Give us the joy to await next year,
when he'll be home, our love to share
When we grow weary carrying life's load,
Cheer us O Lord with your comforting
Word,
Grant us the desire, your Scriptures
to behold
Giving strength and courage as we
traverse life's road
And when the day at last has come,
When all we dreamed came true as
planned,
As we count our blessings every
Setting of the sun,
Hold us safe always in the palm of
Your hand.

1 - A term used in the
Philippines for Overseas
Contract Worker

Gingging

(reprinted from Pinoy Overseas Chronicle, Philippines, November 1991, p.27)

THERE IS STILL HOPE
1992

Painting by Fayez El Abed Al Hasany. From Hamama, born in 1952

Trick or Treat, in Time of Famine

What country may be explored
that dearly loved ones
may live from day to day

is there a space for a woman
aside from domestic work
or amidst cavorting lights
to what country shall a candle be lit

Asia, maybe?
in Singapore? Where Flor was hanged?
Taiwan? A number run to flee,
Malaysia? Thousands are arrested,
Hong Kong? A virus roam infecting the brain,
Japan? Plagued with Hepatitis-B.

Where, oh where?
CNMI? Commonwealth or Northern Marianas Islands?
But women without a stitch are made to walk the streets.

Ah, Australia !
but women are murdered without mercy.

In the Middle East, sooo many Filipinos there
Saudi Arabia, United Arab Emirates
Libya, Oman... Qatar...
But, to bathe quite often is not allowed
or rape becomes inevitable
to complain means either beheading
or lashes and detention

What about Europe?
But, it is quite scary
for one whose nose is cute and small

and there is but a little space
for those whose blood is not as blue

pen, pen de sarapen
de kutsilyo de almasen[1]

Seychelles !
Where in the world is this
to fly overseas or not, is the question.

How, how the carabao
batuten

Ah, tis better to die struggling
than to die with open eyes
and be feasted by flies
'tis said, deeds reside in every person
while mercy comes from God

Aba Ginoong Maria, napupuna ng...
Aba Ginoong...
(Since when did Mary become a Mister)

But what kind of job
awaits overseas?

Domestic Help, may be?
That would be easy
going to the supermarket, cleaning
cooking, cleaning
laundry, cleaning
setting the dining table, cleaning
cleaning the toilet
take a rest.... while baby-sitting.

Guess it is difficult.

An entertainer?
Glittering wardrobes, plunging style

1 - Limericks (except for Aba Ginoong Maria, which is the Hail Mary), probably written as a parody of the English language during US colonization of the Philippines.

that men may even take a peek into the soul
smile to the ears
play dumb to every touch or hug
be ready to undress
undress... undress?

Guess it is difficult.

How about marrying a foreigner
'tis easier to close one's eyes
while ensuring an open purse
they can say anything,
like a Filipina is as cheap as
a second hand car, the hell may care
Mom and Dad, brothers and sis
to nephews and nieces may live
in exchange of an everlasting sacrifice

Guess it is difficult.

Why oh why
must life be this way
when everyone is born naked in this world
the woman who gave birth to humanity
is nailed to do every bidding and giving birth

sipit namimilipit
ginto't pilak namumulaklak
sa tabi ng dagat

if it so happens, against all odds
one decides to be counted
among millions of migrant workers
what will the future hold
in failure and what if in misery
life snaps in the end...

Will the government light a candle
a government that lives off remittances

and a never ending debt from IMF and WB
or will my remains rot in an alien surrounding

what is there to hope for in the midst of despair
from embassy officials who connive with syndicates
and busily fight each other because of *feng shui*
pray tell, is it a sin to cast a spell ?

sayang pula, tatlong pera
sayang puti, tatlong salapi.

NENA GAJUDO FERNANDEZ
"Pitik Bulag sa Panahon ng Tagsalat" (reprinted from T.N.T. trends, news and tidbits,
official newsletter of Kanlungan Centre Foundation, no. 13, April-June 1996, p.24;
translated by Ilena)

LEND ME YOUR EARS

Oh, Our Tamils of Eelam, please listen
Join us, unitedly we will serve our brethren
It is these works and crafts; that
are going to serve us in good stead
When we return to our land and our land blossom rich
and beautiful.

Not only the education we receive in schools alone is education
Even the various Handicrafts we learn is also education
We learn many crafts by merely looking at how they are done,
and when our young women take to these crafts, these crafts attain
a special significance.

Many crafts they learn using palmayrah leaves and turn out useful
    and beautiful products
And when they get back to their land,
Every home will be made into handicraft factory,
And this will keep them going, only working from their homes.

Once the bunches have matured, of the plantation trees
The stem need not be thrown to the garbage pits.
The tissues from the trunks are made use of as fibres to join
    flowers for garlands

Potentialities of these fibres are immense to make textiles of silk
    also, in the world of tomorrow.

Let us learn to cut and stitch garments of various forms.
And instruct the others to do the same and live well, caring for
For our fellow beings
We will engage ourselves in income generation projects,
And we will lift our heads aloft live our lives in grace and dignity –
    our women will give us the lead.

EELATHU RATNAM

Eelathu Ratnam produced Tamil and Sinhala films. In 1983 he fled to Tamil Nadu, India, where he joined, as a volunteer, the Organization of Eelam Refugee Rehabilitation (OfERR). He died in a tragic accident in 1994. The refugees at the camp where he was have continued to use song and poetry to express themselves. (translated from Tamil by V. Kailayapi)